LIBBY LAZEWNIK

and other stories

The Judaica Press, Inc.

Going in Circles and other stories

ISBN: 978-1-60763-072-2

Editor: Miriam Jakubowicz
Proofreader: Hadassa Goldsmith
Cover design and internal layout: Justine Elliott

THE JUDAICA PRESS, INC.
123 Ditmas Avenue / Brooklyn, NY 11218
718-972-6200 / 800-972-6201
info@judaicapress.com
www.judaicapress.com

Manufactured in the United States of America

FOR

Hillel Wainhaus,
Ari Lazewnik
and
Shimi Lazewnik

WITH SO
MUCH LOVE!

Contents

A Word from the Author

Here's the thing about life: It can be frustrating. We strike out on a certain road — only to hit a dead-end.

We make plans — and something happens to upset them.

We make friends, but they don't always turn out the way we hoped.

We make mistakes … and more mistakes … and then some more.

Doesn't it sometimes feel as if we're going in circles?

The funny thing is, even as we keep circling the same old problems, we're also growing. Each time we

run into a similar situation, we're a little older and wiser than we were the time before. We have a better chance of getting things right.

And if we don't … well, there's always the next time! Because life is like that: a circle of experience.

And it's a circle of hearts, all connected to one another. Like the girls in the story that lends its name to this book: I help you to where you need to go, and you help me.

We're a circle of dancers, each moving separately, and yet together forming a single, glorious pattern.

So join the circle … and dance!

Libby Lazewnik

Eyes to See

"**What's** going on?" I whispered to my friend Miriam about ten seconds after I'd walked into our classroom. It was clear as daylight that *something* was going on. Everywhere I looked, small clusters of girls were whispering, their faces anxious and drawn. Most surprising of all, our teacher, Morah Baumgarten, wasn't doing a thing to stop them.

"Morah just made an announcement," Miriam whispered back. "About Kayla. She said —"

I didn't get to hear what my teacher had said, because Morah chose that moment to restore order in the room.

"That's enough, girls. Of course, we're all going to *daven* for Kayla. On the day of her surgery, the whole school will have an assembly and say *Tehillim* for her. But right now, we have some *Chumash* to learn …."

"What surgery?" I whispered frantically.

Miriam gave her head a tiny shake. Morah Baumgarten had her eye on us, and it had that no-nonsense look I knew so well. I bit my tongue.

I can't say I remember much about that *Chumash* lesson. My mind was filled with question marks.

Kayla?

Surgery?

Kayla had been in our class from the very beginning,

but I can't say I was ever especially close to her. I ran with a different circle of friends, and she — well, she seemed to run with hardly any friends at all. It wasn't that anyone disliked her or anything. She was just a quiet, unassuming girl who seemed to enjoy her own company. A loner.

Kayla wore thick glasses and spent a lot of her free time with her nose in a book. That didn't exactly make her suited to the social whirl. But then again, the social whirl did not seem to interest her much. Looking around surreptitiously, I saw that she was absent today.

Surgery?

Never had the recess bell seemed so long in coming. Just when I was absolutely convinced that it had broken down and that class would go on forever — it rang. Morah dismissed us for recess. I twisted in my seat to face Miriam.

"Tell me," I ordered.

"Morah said that Kayla was born with a problem in her eyes," Miriam said slowly. "It seems to have suddenly gotten much worse. The doctor says she has to have a serious operation … or else …"

"Or else?" I prompted.

Miriam was back to a whisper. "She could go blind."

I gasped.

"If the operation doesn't work," Miriam ended sadly, "she could go blind anyway."

Poor Kayla! My heart wrung with pity.

"When is her surgery?" I asked as we started for the door.

"Next week. But she and her parents are flying out to the hospital the day after tomorrow. The doctors want her there a few days early, for tests and things."

I pounced on one word. "Flying?"

Miriam nodded. "The hospital where she's having her operation is in another state — across the country."

Recess passed in a blur. All around me in the schoolyard, girls ran and played or just stood around talking. I did neither. I was too busy thinking about Kayla.

I imagined her being wheeled into the operating room, heart pounding as she said good-bye to her parents and wondered if she'd ever be able to see them again ....

My fists clenched. This was crazy! Such things shouldn't be happening to an ordinary girl in an ordinary class.

But it *was* happening. On the day after tomorrow, Kayla and her parents would be boarding a plane, while the rest of us stayed behind, secure and healthy, with nothing to do but wait. And *daven* ...

Kayla was still on my mind as I walked home that

afternoon. I wanted to talk to my mother about her, but I realized as soon as I walked through the front door that our discussion would have to wait. My mother and middle sister, Yael, were in the midst of a full-scale battle of wills.

"It's just three short blocks," Ma said wearily. "You'll be back in no time."

"But I *hate* walking alone!" Yael wailed. "Can't I just call Debby and see if she can go with me?"

"I don't think you need a friend just to walk over to the grocery store." Ma sounded even more tired than before. "Calling her and then waiting for her to come over will take too much time. I need that cheese so I can finish making supper."

"But —"

"*Please*, Yael."

Yael scowled at the floor. Then she transferred the scowl to her coat and flung it over her shoulders. A moment later she was out the door, closing it behind her just a little harder than strictly necessary.

Ma shook her head and smiled at me. "Hi, Shani. How was your day?"

"How was your day?" a second voice echoed. My little sister, Rina, was on the rug, where — unnoticed by me — she'd been playing with some paper dolls.

"Fine," I said, throwing Rina a hasty smile. I turned

urgently back to my mother. “Ma, a girl in my class — Kayla — has to have a serious operation on her eyes next week. If the surgery doesn’t work, she could go blind!”

Ma paled. “Oh, my. That poor girl … She must be terrified.”

“I’ll bet she is. We’re going to *daven* for her, and the whole school will say *Tehillim* on the day of the surgery.” I sat down next to Ma on the couch. “But I keep feeling that there’s something else we should be doing …”

Ma considered the issue. “At times like this, it’s always considered a good idea to take on an extra mitzvah or *chesed* — something to earn a *zechus* for Kayla’s recovery.”

My eyes lit up. “That’s a great idea! I’ll tell Morah Baumgarten about it tomorrow. Maybe our whole class can take on something extra.”

“That sounds wonderful, Shani. And please don’t forget to tell me her name so I can say *Tehillim*, too.” There’s something about my mother’s smile that makes me feel warm inside even in January. I basked in it for a few minutes, and then headed for my room to get some homework out of the way.

For some reason, I couldn’t concentrate. With Ma’s suggestion tucked into my schoolbag, so to speak, I should have felt satisfied. We were doing all that we could for Kayla. The rest was up to Hashem.

But — were we? No matter how I tried to push it away, the question kept intruding, niggling at me like some annoying pest. There must be something else we could do for Kayla. But I had no idea what it was.

Kayla was absent the next day, too. I wouldn't be seeing her again until after her operation. I wondered how she was feeling today. Then I realized that there was no need to wonder. I knew exactly how she was feeling, because it was the same way *I'd* be feeling if I were in her shoes.

Terrified.

Somehow the day passed, though it seemed to crawl on legs of lead. I talked to Miriam about Kayla at recess, and talked about her some more at lunch. She was never far from my thoughts as I sat through one endless class after another. When the bell finally rang to release me from what had begun to feel like a life sentence, I shot out of my seat.

"What's your rush?" Miriam asked as she began unhurriedly to stuff things into her schoolbag.

"I don't know." I shrugged. "I'm feeling restless today." Kayla's operation was hanging over my head, just as surely as it was hanging over hers.

On the spot, I decided that I wouldn't wait for next week's assembly to say *Tehillim* for Kayla. I was going to start saying it the minute I got home from school.

I hoped that it would help her — but I *knew* that it would help me!

Yael was having a study sleepover at her friend Debby's that night. Her bed was empty as I went into the room she shared with Rina. I found my little sister curled up under the blanket, looking sleepy and wide-awake at the same time.

"Hi, Rina. Ma's kind of busy, so she asked me to read you your bedtime story tonight. Okay?"

Rina nodded. I pulled out a book, perched at the edge of her bed and started reading.

I took my time over the story, to give Rina a chance to get really drowsy. It seemed to work. When I closed the book at last, I leaned down and gave her a kiss. "Let's say *Shema* now, okay? And then you can go to sleep."

A couple of minutes later, I switched off the light and closed the door softly behind me. Rina was down for the night ....

Or that's what I thought.

I had just opened a notebook and was about to tackle some math problems when my bedroom door swung silently open. In the doorway stood a woebegone figure in flannel pajamas and a pair of furry slippers.

"Rina!" I exclaimed in surprise. "What's the matter?"

"I can't sleep," she said in a small voice. "My room is too big."

"Too big? It's the same size as always!"

"It's too big without Yael in it," she explained, pattering over to my bed and climbing in. "And also too dark. I want to sleep here, with you."

"But I'm doing my homework! Won't the light bother you?"

"Nope," she said simply.

I tried one more time. "Rina, I really think you'll sleep better in your own bed."

Her eyes filled. "But I'm scared of being all alone in the dark. I want Ya-e-e-el!"

"Okay, okay. You can stay." Thankfully, the tears dried up as quickly as they'd come. I tucked her in and gave her another kiss. A moment later, the sound of soft, even breathing told me that Rina was really sound asleep this time.

I switched off the overhead light and used my desk lamp for my homework instead. But the math could not hold my attention. Something was tickling the back of my brain, and try as I might, I couldn't ignore it.

I'm scared of being all alone in the dark.

I hate walking alone ....

My room is too big without Yael ....

I sat up so abruptly that my head spun. That was *exactly* what Kayla must be feeling tonight, as she prepared to fly away to a strange hospital tomorrow for an operation that could make such a huge difference in her life — one way or another.

Not just terrified.

Alone.

"Nobody should be alone at a time like this," I whispered.

That was what I decided as I sat staring sightlessly down at my notebook in the yellow circle of lamplight, as my little sister lay softly sleeping in the bed behind me.

The flight was scheduled for six p.m., which meant that they had to be at the airport at least an hour before that. Kayla and her mother carried their carry-on luggage to the car parked in the driveway. Her father, at the wheel, had already stowed the heavier suitcases in the trunk and was seated behind the wheel waiting for them.

Kayla turned to take one last look at her house. Was this the last time she would ever see it? Swallowing a lump, she told herself not to think that way. She *would* get better. The operation was going to work. Hashem would help her. He had to!

Her mother seemed to sense how she was feeling. In fact, she was feeling much the same way herself .... She put her arm around her daughter and gave her a quick hug before they both stepped into the car. Kayla's father backed carefully out of the driveway and turned down the street.

Kayla craned her neck for a last glimpse of her block. And then they were on other streets, moving toward the highway that would take them to the airport. Beyond that, she didn't want to think. She didn't want to think about the plane that would bear her away from the city where she'd grown up, and bring her to a strange hospital in a strange place, where a strange doctor would do scary things to her eyes.

She didn't want to think about it, because thinking about it made the lump in her throat grow even bigger. Soon it would be too big to contain, and then she would embarrass herself — a big seventh-grader — by breaking down in tears.

Nobody talked much on the way to the airport.

They carried their bags over to the correct counter

and waited in line. Kayla glanced idly around as she waited for her father to check them in and for their baggage to be weighed.

"Hey!" she exclaimed suddenly.

"What?" her mother asked, her attention focused on what the airline clerk was saying.

"There's someone I know. I wonder where *she's* going?"

"Who?" her mother asked absently, as her husband accepted their boarding passes.

"Someone from my class …" Kayla's eyes widened. "Wait — there's someone else! What …?" She blinked hard. "I don't believe this …."

Something in Kayla's voice caught her mother's attention. She turned away from the counter and followed Kayla's gaze.

Her own eyes grew as wide as her daughter's. Suddenly speechless, she clutched Kayla's hand and stared through eyes that were suddenly blurred with unstoppable tears.

I waved. "Hi, Kayla!"

Behind me, the three girls who'd come along in our car waved, too. And behind them, the girls who'd come in other cars began streaming in, waving and smiling

at Kayla, who stood transfixed beside her mother near the airline counter.

Kayla's father turned from the counter, boarding passes in hand. He froze in astonishment.

Through the automatic doors came the rest of our class, in a long, steady stream. Down the terminal from the right came Morah Baumgarten, accompanied by her husband and children. My own parents and the other parents who had driven us crowded in behind us. Some were pushing strollers or leading toddlers by the hand. And here came Rabbi Mendelson, our principal, holding onto his hat as he flew threw the sliding doors.

"Did I make it?" he gasped. "Am I too late?"

"You're not too late," I assured him. "Kayla's still here." And we all turned to smile at Kayla.

"We came to see you off," I said — somewhat unnecessarily, I thought. But I had to say something. Kayla was staring as if she'd just seen a ghost. A few dozen ghosts …

"You came," Kayla repeated, as if she couldn't believe it.

"Of course we did!" I said. "Nobody should be alone at a time like this."

Kayla's mother lunged forward and enveloped me in a hug. When she released me — my face felt as red as a ripe tomato — I saw that Kayla felt like doing the same thing. Something in her face that had been tight and closed seemed to open up, like a flower in the sun. She smiled.

"Thanks," she said softly. Her voice sounded a bit choked. "This is amazing."

"*You're* amazing," I said. "We're all rooting for you, Kayla. You're going to come through this with flying colors. I just know it."

"This was all Shani's idea," Morah Baumgarten told Kayla and her parents.

"I let your whole class out of school early," Rabbi Mendelson added, to show Kayla the honor she'd rated.

Kayla turned pink. "Thank you — all of you. This is … amazing," she repeated. She couldn't seem to think of any other word.

"*Refuah sheleimah*," Morah said. She stepped back so that Kayla could see us all: principal and teacher and classmates and parents, and the sprinkling of younger siblings who'd come along for the ride.

"*Refuah sheleimah*, Kayla," we chorused. "Come back soon. We'll miss you!"

Kayla looked at us as though she was drinking us in. As though memorizing every detail.

"I'll be back as soon as I can," she promised.

She was wearing a smile as she followed her parents

to the security gate, waving good-bye to us again and again.

And she was smiling as she walked into our classroom, some three weeks later.

"Kayla!" Morah Baumgarten exclaimed, breaking off in mid-sentence.

"Hi, Morah," Kayla said, beaming shyly at her, and at all of us. "It's good to be here." She drew a deep breath. "It's great to *see* all of you again …."

I let out a breath that I seemed to have been holding for the past three weeks.

And then — under our teacher's approving gaze — our whole class surged forward like the spring tide, to welcome Kayla home.

A Pebble of Hope

Mordy held his breath and peeked out from behind the big oak tree. There they were! His two older cousins, Naftali and Zev, had just come out of the main building and were sauntering away together, talking a mile a minute as they went.

Naftali and Zev were the same age — three years older than Mordy — and they always had a lot to say to each other when they were together. This family reunion had provided them with a perfect opportunity.

Zeidy and Bubby had brought the whole family together to this hotel for the weekend. Mordy loved talking with his *zeidy*, but a kid couldn't do that all day. A kid wanted to play with other kids. Unfortunately, when Naftali and Zev were together, they were uninterested in anyone else — least of all, pesky younger cousins.

Still, Mordy was determined. All of his other cousins were younger than he was, or were girls. Naftali and Zev had made it very clear that they were not eager to have him tag along — which was why Mordy was skulking behind trees. Maybe if he popped out suddenly when they were walking along, they would let him join them.

Not likely, but possible … Mordy would have preferred better odds, but if he couldn't have a rock of hope to lean on, he'd settle for a pebble ....

The older boys were walking along the path under the shady trees. Deep in conversation, they didn't notice the smaller figure trotting along behind them. Mordy felt like a secret agent as he shadowed his quarry. He slipped from tree to tree, never letting them out of his sight.

"So, what do you think?" Naftali asked Zev, as the two dropped down to the grass beneath a tall tree with spreading branches. The leaves above their heads danced in a light breeze, making the leaf-shadows dance on the ground below.

Zev opened his mouth to tell Naftali what he thought — but he never had the chance. Mordy had decided to make his move.

"Hi!" he called, popping out from behind the very tree the older cousins had been sheltering under. "Whatcha doing?"

Avoiding you, his cousins might have said. Instead, with a wry exchange of glances, they told him, "We've got some stuff to discuss, Mordy."

"Private stuff," Zev said meaningfully.

"You can join us later, if you want," Naftali added as he saw the disappointment in the younger boy's eyes.

"Yeah. Later," Mordy repeated dully. "Later" always meant "never." He tried one last time to appeal to their softer side. "I'm so bored. I have no one to play with."

"Later," Zev said firmly.

Head down, Mordy shuffled away. The cousins watched him go. As soon as he was out of earshot, they resumed their conversation.

Mordy didn't go far. The prospect of hanging around all by himself for the rest of the afternoon was not a happy one. He hovered on the path several yards away from the older boys, looking like a dejected but hopeful puppy.

Zev was annoyed. Cupping his hands around his mouth, he shouted, "Hey, Mordy! I think your mother wants you!"

Mordy glanced back in the direction of the hotel, and then shook his head.

"See you later. Okay?" Naftali called.

Mordy nodded, but did not budge. He kicked at the gravel path and gave them some more puppy-dog looks.

Naftali found it hard to ignore those pleading eyes. Zev found it hard to talk to Naftali with their younger cousin forming a distraction. At last, he stood up.

"C'mon, Naftali. Let's find some place where we won't be haunted by pests."

With an apologetic look over his shoulder, Naftali followed Zev down the path.

•◎•◎•

"Look at that shed," Zev said, pointing. "Wonder what's inside?"

"Only one way to find out," said Naftali. They started forward.

The shed was on the extreme edge of the hotel's grounds, adjacent to a wild patch of bushes and other undergrowth. Beyond this patch were trees — many of them. A forest. The shed was the last stop before the wilderness.

It wasn't much to look at. Peeling brown paint was its only decoration. The ancient shack looked as if a strong gust of wind could knock it over. But on the door hung a surprisingly strong, new-looking padlock.

"Door's locked," Zev said unnecessarily.

"Let's look through the windows." Shading his eyes with his hands, Naftali peered through the dirty glass — and saw nothing. The windows had been boarded up on the inside.

"There's nothing to see," Naftali said, turning away. "C'mon, let's go back and find something to eat. I'm starving!"

Though they'd enjoyed a hearty lunch an hour ago, Zev had no argument with this. Just before he, too, turned away from the shack, he reached up and gave the shiny new padlock a half-hearted tug.

To his surprise, it fell open!

The loop of the lock had not been firmly latched in its hole. Zev's touch had detached the loop from the rest of the lock, leaving it hanging temptingly on the rusted rectangle of metal.

With one accord, the boys plucked the lock out of the latch and pulled the door ajar. It opened with a creak of protesting hinges.

Naftali and Zev poked their heads through the doorway, but the boarded-up windows made it too dark to see. Cautiously, they stepped inside.

"It's probably used for storing things," Naftali said as they picked their way through a mass of wooden crates. "Lawn mowers, gardening tools — stuff like that."

But there was no "stuff like that" to be seen. Only crates — and more crates. Zev glanced at the writing on one of them. Now that his eyes had become accustomed to the dimness, the light coming in through the open door was enough to read by.

"'Fragile,'" he read. "And 'This Side Up.' Wonder what's in these?"

"Look, here's one with the top open," Naftali said. Moved by idle curiosity, he pushed aside the wooden lid of the nearest box and peered inside. "Hey, look at this!"

"Let me see." Zev leaned over the box beside Naftali.

Lined up in neat rows inside the crate, like glass soldiers on parade, were a dozen elegant, cork-topped bottles.

"It's champagne, I think," Zev said, picking up a bottle and studying it. "The label's in French."

"Why would boxes of French champagne be sitting in a rickety old shed at the edge of nowhere?" Naftali wondered aloud.

"It's not the edge of nowhere," Zev reminded him. "It's the edge of the hotel grounds. These must belong to the hotel."

"But wouldn't they store champagne someplace more convenient — like the cellar? Isn't that where wine is usually kept? Why out here?"

It was a good question. Zev and Naftali had hiked a good long way before they'd seen this shcd. Why store such expensive stuff — and Zev was sure, from the look of those bottles, that they cost a lot — way out here, practically in the woods?

"For safe-keeping?" he asked.

"Nah. The hotel cellars would be much more secure."

Both boys gazed at the bottle in Zev's hand, as though it might pop its cork at any minute and give them the answer. But the bottle kept its secrets.

Zev froze. "*Shh!* I hear someone …."

Deftly, he slipped the bottle back into its crate. Without a word, both boys slipped into the deepest, darkest corner of the shed, behind a tall pile of wooden crates. They held their breaths.

Even before they saw the men, they heard their voices.

"Hey! Who left the door open?" one of them asked. He sounded angry and scared at the same time.

"It wasn't me," said another voice. "I locked it good and tight when I brought in the latest delivery."

"I'll bet you forgot."

"I didn't!"

"So *you* say …"

"Why would I forget to lock the door when I know that if this stuff's found, we head right for jail? Think I'd be so stupid?"

The other man didn't bother answering. He began prowling around the shed, checking on the merchandise. He stopped short of the tall pile of crates in the darkest corner.

"Everything seems to be okay. Maybe the lock wasn't closed all the way, and the wind swung the door open."

"Maybe." The second voice sounded relieved. "We're

lucky no one comes out here."

"Not usually," the first voice reminded him. "But it could happen. We can't afford to take chances."

There was a brief silence, as though both of them were thinking of a prison cell.

"Okay. This stuff's ready to go tonight," the first voice announced. "What time did Joe say he'd be here with the truck?"

"Midnight. We're supposed to be waiting by the road to lead him here with the dolly."

"Let's see … Five crates on the dolly each trip … Five minutes per trip to and from the truck … That should clear the shed in about half an hour."

"Yep. Twelve-thirty or so, we're tucked up in our beds — and no one's the wiser," the second voice agreed.

"And *we're* five thousand dollars richer!"

"Each."

"Each," the first voice repeated in a tone of supreme satisfaction.

There was a sound that could only come from hands rubbing gleefully together. "Now, tell me this wasn't a brainstorm I had. We're gonna be rich, you and me!"

"Selling hotel champagne to Joe …"

"Every penny of it clear profit …"

Suddenly, the second voice sounded worried. "Hey,

it's getting late. Gotta get back to the kitchen, or the cook'll have my head."

"And I've gotta set those tables. Let's go!"

"One of these days, we'll have enough to quit these dead-end jobs," the second voice said as they left the shed. "And then I'll tell that cook where to get off …"

The door closed with a firm thud. This was quickly followed by an audible click as the padlock was engaged. The voices faded away.

Zev put a finger to his lips and motioned for Naftali to stay where he was. Quiet as mice, the cousins remained motionless behind the pile of crates. At last, when Zev deemed it safe, he rose creakily to his feet.

"Did you hear that?" he whispered.

Naftali nodded solemnly. "Those guys are crooks. Selling the hotel's champagne!"

Zev looked around. "We've got to get out of here — warn someone about their plans!"

A very quick tour of the cramped shed showed them that there was no way out. The windows were boarded up and the door securely locked. They were trapped!

Naftali thought of something else. "If we're still here when they come back at midnight …"

The cousins stared at each other in the darkness. A sliver of daylight between two of the boards on the window allowed Naftali to see Zev's face. He wondered if his own was just as pale.

"Maybe someone else will come by," he said, the words sounding more cheerful than he felt. "We can yell."

"Go ahead and yell your head off," Zev said gloomily. "Out here at the edge of nowhere — who'll hear us?"

It was at that moment that they heard the sound at the window.

It was a rattling sound, as though something small and hard had been flung at the glass.

That's just what it had been. Mordy, hiding behind the shed that his cousins had entered, had grown tired of waiting for them to come out. From his place of concealment, he'd heard some men's voices. Then he heard his cousins talking again. But Zev and Naftali did not seem ready to come out anytime soon. Apparently, they were still intent on avoiding his company.

Disgruntled, he threw a pebble at one of the windows. He regretted it a moment later. He didn't want his cousins to know he'd been waiting all this time …. He trotted dejectedly away down the path. Let them stay in that stupid old shed if they wanted to. He'd go back to the hotel and find Zeidy. Zeidy always had time to talk to him.

Inside the shed, the cousins waited tensely for a repeat of the sound. Had it been a stray twig that knocked against the window — or a human presence who might help them out of this impasse?

The sound was not repeated. Still, as they sat in the darkness praying for rescue, the sound stayed with Naftali and Zev, like a small, glad ray of light in the gloom.

Like a pebble of hope.

It took Mordy some time to track down his *zeidy*. He found him at last in a corner of the lobby, a big Gemara open on the table before him.

"Mordy!" His grandfather marked his page and closed the Gemara. "I haven't seen you around for a while. What have you been doing with yourself since lunch?"

Mordy perched gloomily on a chair. "What I usually do at family reunions. Try to get Naftali and Zev to play with me."

"They didn't?"

He shook his head. "They wouldn't even look at me! They think I'm too young for them."

"That," Zeidy said with a twinkle, "is a problem that time always solves."

This did not cheer Mordy much.

"They were so eager to get away from me that they ran and hid in an old shed near the woods! I waited a long time, but they didn't come out."

"Oh?" Zeidy frowned. "They shouldn't be going into places like that. Are you sure they didn't come out?"

"They probably did, the minute I left," Mordy said. He propped his chin on his fists, the picture of misery. "There were a couple of big guys there for a while, too. And then *they* left. But not the cousins."

"A couple of big guys." Slowly, Zeidy straightened in his chair. "I don't like the sound of that."

"Neither do I. That Zev and Naftali never want to spend any time with me! They think that just 'cause they're older, they can —"

"Come with me." To Mordy's surprise, Zeidy was on his feet.

Obediently, he trotted after his grandfather to a room that had "Security" written on the door.

Wondering, he followed his *zeidy* inside.

Naftali had fallen into a light doze. In his dream, he and Zeidy were walking in the woods.

"Listen," Zeidy said. "Hear that sound? That's a woodpecker."

Naftali heard the tap-tap-tap. It went on and on. "That's one busy bird," he laughed. And still the tapping continued. Tap-tap-tap …

"Hey, Naftali," Zev whispered, prodding him in the ribs. "Someone's knocking on the window!"

And then came the sweetest sound of all: Zeidy's voice — their real *zeidy*, not a figure of a dream, calling softly, "Naftali? Zev? Are you in there?"

"ZEIDY!" Both cousins were scrambling over crates, banging shins and scraping elbows in their haste to reach the window. "We're here, Zeidy! Please get us out!"

They heard a murmur of voices on the other side. Then an unfamiliar male voice called, "I'll just get something to break that padlock, boys. I'm leaving one of my men here on guard. Stay put!"

"Where does he think we're going?" Zev giggled, on the edge of hysteria.

Naftali just smiled and lifted his eyes heavenward, whispering, "Thank You, Hashem."

There was someone else to thank, too. When they were safely outside and reunited with Zeidy and a hotel security team, they saw Mordy, hanging back shyly at the edges of the small group. But there was no chance to say anything. One of the security guards questioned them about the men who had locked them inside — while the others were examining the contents of the shed with great interest.

"The kitchen, you said?" the guard repeated. "He mentioned that he was going back to the kitchen?"

"One of them said he was," Zev said patiently. "The other one said he had to set the tables."

"A waiter." The head guard met his colleague's eye. He turned to Zeidy. "Why don't you take these boys back to the hotel? I'm sure they could use a drink and something to eat, after that ordeal."

"What are you going to do about those crooks?" Zeidy asked.

"We'll have a team ready and waiting here at midnight," the head guard said. "Those men aren't going to be selling — or drinking — champagne for a long, long time ...."

Zev and Naftali started slowly back to the main building with their grandfather.

"Where's Mordy?" Naftali asked suddenly. "I saw him before, but he's not here now."

"I think he's a little embarrassed," Zeidy said in a gentle voice.

"Embarrassed? Why?" Both cousins were mystified.

"Seems he hung around that shed for a long time,

waiting for you to come out. He doesn't want you to know that. You seem to think he's a pest or something." Zeidy lifted a questioning brow.

Both boys had the grace to look ashamed. "I guess we didn't exactly treat him well," Naftali said. "I'm going to apologize."

"*And* thank him," Zev said. "He's the one who got us rescued!"

•◎•◎•

It took the cousins a while to find Mordy. This afternoon, he didn't want to be found. At last, they tracked him down under a tree near the pool. Naftali and Zev flanked him, one on either side. They thanked the younger boy for his help, which he shrugged off.

"That's okay," Mordy said, looking down at the ground. "You can go now. I know you don't really want to hang around with me."

"We're not budging until you tell us you forgive us," Naftali said staunchly. And Zev chimed in, "Not one step!"

Slowly, a smile dawned on Mordy's face. "You mean, you'll stay right here with me until I say you're forgiven?"

Both cousins nodded.

Mordy's smile grew even bigger. The situation had

interesting possibilities ….

Judging by the expressions on his cousins' faces, he didn't think he'd have much trouble with their ignoring him in the future. The tiny pebble of hope had turned into a gigantic boulder on which he could safely rest his fondest dreams.

"Okay, then," he said happily. "First we'll play catch, and then basketball, and then, after supper …"

Smile!

Here's how I spent the first hour of my Monday morning: growling at my brother, snapping at my sister, scowling at my other sister, and generally being anything but a ray of sunshine. By the time I got down to the kitchen for breakfast, half my family was mad at me and the other half was scared they'd be next.

"Good morning, Aviva," my mother greeted me. "I've got hot cereal for you, if you'd like some. And you'd better bundle up today — it's very cold out."

I was about to say, "Yes, please," but I never got the chance. My brother Eli burst into the kitchen in his usual noisy fashion, talking as he came.

"Ma, I can't find my homework! I did it last night — you *saw* me do it — but now it's gone! And my teacher's gonna kill me if I don't have it today, because he warned me the last time I forgot. Only, this time, I *didn't* forget! I did it! You *saw* me do it with your own eyes, right? Do you think you could write a note for my teacher?"

What Ma would have answered I'll never know, because my youngest sister, Fraidy, chose that moment to splash some of the milk from her bowl right onto my foot.

"YOW! Fraidy, what are you doing?" I yelled.

"It was an accident," Fraidy said, lip quivering.

"Well, thanks a lot! Now I have to go back upstairs and change my socks. Can't you be a *little* more careful?"

Fraidy burst into tears.

Eli was still talking. "Mr. Stein is going to be *so-o-o* mad, Ma! Can't I *please* have a note?"

Ma gathered Fraidy into her arms to soothe her, saying over her head, "I'm sure your homework can be found, Eli. Where did you look?"

"EVERYWHERE!" Eli announced dramatically. His voice grated on my already frazzled nerves, so I stood up and snapped, "Would you *mind* turning down the decibel level just a notch? Some of us don't care to start the day with a headache!"

"You're talking just as loud as me!" Eli shot back, momentarily diverted from his homework crisis.

My father walked into the kitchen. Ma, her arms still full of Fraidy, gave him an imploring look.

"What's the problem?" Abba asked.

"Aviva yelled at me," Fraidy sniffled into Ma's shoulder.

"Aviva yelled at *me*," Eli pouted.

"Aviva," Abba said quietly, "can you step outside with me for a minute?"

I followed him into the living room, where I sat down on the sofa with a pointed thud. "This is so

unfair," I said. "*They* drive me crazy — and *I* get all the blame!"

Abba regarded me in silence for a few seconds, during which I began to feel rather uncomfortable. Finally, he said, "Smile, Aviva."

"Huh?" I was startled.

"Give me a smile. Give the world a smile. You'd be surprised at what a difference it makes."

I regarded my father suspiciously. "You're kidding, right?"

"Absolutely not. It's much harder to snap at someone when you're wearing a smile." He paused. "In fact, it's harder to *feel* like snapping at someone. So, come on — smile!"

Reluctantly, I forced my lips into a ghastly grin. "Like this?"

"Not bad — for a start. Work on it, Aviva. Don't let little things get under your skin. Don't let your sisters and brothers push your buttons. Stop yourself before you lash into people and hurt their feelings."

I sighed. "I try, Abba. I really do. I'm thirteen years old, and it feels like I've been trying all my life. You've spoken to me about this before. Ma's spoken to me about it, too. I speak to *myself* about it — all the time! But none of it seems to stick. That's the honest truth."

Abba gestured at the window, where a light snow was falling. "That snow doesn't look like it's going to stick, either. But with enough time and perseverance, it will. Keep trying, Aviva. You'll get there. I have confidence in you."

Which was more than I could say about myself.

I kept that fake grin stretched across my face as I returned to the kitchen. It remained ludicrously — and uselessly — in place as I ate my cereal, growled at my brother, snapped at my sister, muttered "Good-bye" to my mother, and stomped out the door to school.

School was different. With my friends, I rarely had to struggle to hold onto my temper. *They* didn't "push my buttons" the way my family did. Once I'd put a few blocks between myself and my home, I found my spirits rising. By the time I walked into my classroom, I was looking — if not yet like a ray of sunshine — like far less of a thundercloud.

My good mood lasted all the way home. As I walked up the front path, I remembered my conversation with Abba that morning. I resolved to be pleasant to everyone for the rest of the day.

With that worthwhile resolution in hand, I pushed open the door and walked into a scene of mayhem.

The baby had just finished scattering a box of crayons all over the living room rug. Eli and my youngest brother, Shloimy, were roller-blading across the living room, crushing crayons as they went.

"Eli!" I screeched. "LOOK WHAT YOU'RE DOING TO THE FLOOR!"

Eli looked down. "What?"

"You're crushing the crayons into the carpet! Wait till Ma sees this!"

"Oops." Carefully, Eli sidestepped a purple crayon that his rollerblade had been on the point of pulverizing. "Guess we'll have to clean it up. C'mon, Shloimy." He sat down to unstrap his blades.

"You'd better do a good job," I glowered. With a snort, I added a disgusted postscript: "*Boys!*"

Fraidy came into the room, took one look at the mess and started wailing. "My crayons! Ma-a-a! The baby threw my crayons all over the floor! And the boys smashed them all to bits!" Her wails reached a crescendo.

"For heaven's sake, Fraidy," I snapped. "You don't have to make such a fuss. I'll get you some new crayons if you want."

This had the effect of drying some, but not all, of the tears. "But I liked *these* crayons! Why can't Esti play with her own stuff?"

“She’s just a baby,” I explained, barely holding onto my patience.

“So’s Fraidy,” Shloimy taunted.

“No, I’m not!” Fraidy shouted, starting to cry again.

“Sure you are. You’re crying, aren’t you? So you’re a baby. A cry-baby!”

My sister’s howls started the baby whimpering. I put my hands over my ears and stormed out of the room, yelling, “Ma! MA! I need some earplugs. This place is nuts!”

Ma came downstairs, asking, “What’s the trouble?”

“Those kids — they’re the trouble. The boys have made a huge mess, and Fraidy and the baby are making a huge racket. I’m getting out of here!”

Ma let me go, but she tracked me down in my room afterwards. “Aviva, you’re the oldest. A pleasant word from you would have defused the whole situation down there. Why do you have to scream at your brothers and sisters all the time? It just makes everything worse.”

“They drive me nuts,” I grumbled.

“Just try to be pleasant,” she sighed. “You’d be amazed at the results.”

Abba had told me to smile. Ma was telling me to be pleasant. Both things felt as far away from me as the moon.

How could I smile and act pleasantly with such a bunch of siblings? Impossible! And that's the honest truth.

On that discouraging thought, I got out my homework and tried to concentrate on solving math problems. In the peaceful quiet, my jangled nerves began to settle. I was feeling relaxed and content when Fraidy poked her head into my room. "Dinner's ready!"

I jumped. "Fraidy! How many times do I have to ask you to knock before you barge in? You scared me out of my wits!"

"You don't have to y-yell at me," she retorted, lower lip quivering.

"Sure I do! If I don't yell, how will you ever learn to do things right?"

Having no answer for this, Fraidy withdrew in a hurry. I closed my books and followed her downstairs, where I spent most of the dinner hour trying to keep my temper in check as my annoying brothers and sisters spilled drinks, dropped food (on my skirt!), and made enough noise for an army.

"Aviva, could you pass the salt?" Eli asked.

"I'll pass you the salt if *you* stop kicking me under the table every other second!"

Eli looked affronted. "I only did it once. And it was an accident."

"Twice," I said. I thumped the saltshaker on the table in front of him. "And you *might* remember to say 'please.'"

"*You* might remember to smile," Abba murmured, for my ears alone.

But even a fake grin felt like too much trouble just then. I frowned instead, and pointedly said nothing else until the meal was over.

The streets were plowed by morning, and we all left for school as usual. Then, in the afternoon, it started snowing again. The wind picked up, making the snow fly. The city made some urgent announcements about hazardous driving conditions, and school was dismissed early. Happily, our heads down against the driving, snow-filled wind, we made our way home.

When I got there, the house was empty.

"Ma? Someone? Is anyone home?"

Silence.

I went into the kitchen, where I found a hastily-scrawled note in my mother's handwriting.

"*Abba's car skidded on the road and there was an accident. He's in the hospital now. I'll call you when I know more. The others are at the Sheinmans', but the family's going out this evening. Please bring the kids home and keep an eye on them till I get back.*"

I stared at the note in shock. Abba — in an accident? In the *hospital*? How badly was he hurt? My heart began slamming against my rib cage in hard, painful strokes. How long I stood there, I don't know. What roused me at last was the phone. It was ringing.

Mechanically, as if in a dream, I reached out for the receiver.

"Aviva? Is that you?"

"Ma!" All at once, I woke up. "How's Abba?"

"They're about to wheel him into surgery. He's bleeding internally and they don't know how serious it is yet. I'll call you as soon as I know .... Are the kids home?"

"I — I was about to get them."

"Please hurry, Aviva. The Sheinmans have a family wedding to attend tonight and they'll be anxious to leave."

"Okay. We'll *daven* for Abba, Ma. Please call back soon!"

"I will, *bli neder*," she said. "Don't worry, sweetie. It'll be okay."

With those words to give me strength, I went back outside into the snow and battled the wind to our next-door neighbors' house. Ten minutes later I was herding my two brothers and Fraidy back to our house, baby Esti clutched in my arms. By the time we were stamping the snow off our boots inside our own front door, I was exhausted.

And the wait had just begun.

In their worry about Abba, my brothers were not exactly what you'd call well-behaved that night. They kept horsing around, making dumb jokes and teasing Fraidy, until I thought I'd go out of my mind.

But I couldn't go out of my mind — not even a little bit. I couldn't snap or scream or do any of the usual things I did when my siblings pushed my buttons. Ma and Abba were depending on me.

When Fraidy cried — which she did every five minutes or so throughout the evening — I held her in my arms the way I'd seen Ma do. When Eli and Shloimy had a contest to see who could reach the highest note, I felt as if my temper was about to explode along with my eardrums.

But I didn't let it. I couldn't. Abba was in the hospital and Ma was with him. If this house was to retain any semblance of peace and normalcy, it was all up to me.

Thinking of Abba made me remember to smile. Even though my father couldn't see me, I wanted to make him proud. I glued a smile onto my face and refused to let it slip.

"You look funny," Fraidy remarked, in a lull between bouts of crying.

"Funny? What do you mean?"

"Your face looks different." She shrugged. "Can I have more ketchup?" And she went back to eating the noodles that I'd cooked for the kids' dinner.

Somehow, I got them all into bed. The baby fell asleep right away, but the others were not so lucky. Going into their rooms to check on them later, I found Shloimy and Eli whispering anxiously across the room to each other, and Fraidy crying softly into her pillow.

"All right," I sighed. "Everybody up. We'll say some more *Tehillim* for Abba and then play a game."

After we said *Tehillim*, I got out the game of Life. As I laid out the board, I couldn't help thinking that real life is a lot more work than moving a plastic marker around a board and picking the right card. And the hardest part of all is doing the opposite of what everything inside you is clamoring to do … like snapping, and growling, and giving free rein to jangling nerves and an uncertain temper.

When the phone rang, we were in the middle of the game and trying to pretend that we were concentrating. All four of us leaped up, but I got there first. "Ma?"

"Aviva." She sounded very tired.

"How's Abba?" I held my breath.

"*Baruch Hashem*. They found the damage that was causing the bleeding and repaired it. He's still in the recovery room, but they say it went well. Hopefully, you'll be able to visit him tomorrow."

I let out my breath in a long whoosh of air. "Excuse me a second, Ma. I want to tell the kids."

"What — they're still up? It's nearly eleven!"

"They couldn't sleep," I said softly.

When I told my siblings the good news, Fraidy promptly burst into relieved tears, while my brothers began capering around the room, whooping like Indians. This time, neither the tears nor the noise bothered me in the least. I was so filled with gratitude, so joyous down to the bottom of my heart, that nothing else mattered.

And I smiled. I smiled so hard that I almost thought I saw the room fill with sunshine, even though it was the middle of the night and snow lay thickly on the ground outside. It seems that you can create your own weather, wherever you are.

And that's the honest truth.

Three-in-One

Ari woke to the sound of the window panes in his room rattling like chattering teeth.

He blinked his eyes, shook his head to clear it, and looked out the window. Beyond the shaking glass he saw the tree in his backyard waving frantically in the wind. Scraps of newspaper danced into his line of vision and then danced away again. An especially strong gust shook the tree's bare branches so hard that a few twigs broke off and flew away.

Ari's eyes widened. "What a wind!" he exclaimed softly.

He bounced out of bed, energized by all the movement outside his window. He didn't like walking to school in the rain — but a good, strong wind was exciting. Ari was dressed and ready in record time that morning.

There was another reason for his high spirits. His rebbi, Rabbi Morgenstern, had given him an important job: collecting money from his fellow classmates for the end-of-year trip. Rebbi had told him to collect the money as quickly as possible so he could organize the trip. The deadline was this morning. Ari had promised to come through.

Yesterday, he'd collected the last ten dollar bill from the last boy. Today, he would proudly hand the whole amount over to Rabbi Morgenstern. Rebbi would be proud of him. Just thinking of it made Ari's face tingle, as though it was already beginning to blush at all the praise Rebbi would heap on his head.

Before leaving for yeshivah, Ari checked three times to make sure that the envelope with the cash was tucked safely into his knapsack. Then, with a cheery "Bye!" to his mother, he opened the door — and was nearly carried away by the wind.

He quickly regained his balance and started walking. None of the other kids on his block seemed to be around. This was not surprising, as Ari had left home a full half hour earlier than he usually did. Head slightly lowered, he moved doggedly ahead, buffeted by the gusts.

All went well until he reached the part of his walk where he caught his first glimpse of the school building. The sight of the familiar brick structure made him remember where he was going, and what he was going to do when he got there. The envelope he'd so carefully tended these past weeks — counting the bills each evening and pursuing laggard classmates each day — was about to be handed over to his teacher. It had been fun being in charge of such an important job.

As he reached the school gates, Ari felt a sudden urge to look through the envelope one more time before it passed out of his possession. He took off his knapsack and tugged at the zipper. The envelope met his questing fingers. He pulled it out. Ari removed the money and began counting the bills one last time.

Anyone might have told him that this was a big mistake. As careful as he was, he was simply no match for the wind.

An especially powerful gust came by just as he was finishing the counting. With no effort at all, it snatched the last bill out of his fingers. Ari let out a yell and watched in dismay as the bill went spiraling away and out of sight.

If you've ever been on a roller coaster that dropped before you were ready, you know just how Ari felt. From the happy heights of a moment before, he thudded right down into the pit of despair. It was a twenty dollar bill that had flown away from him. Now, instead of being able to hand his rebbi the total amount he'd collected, he'd be forced to admit that the sum was short. Twenty whole dollars short.

A quick survey of the street and the school yard verified the awful truth: The money was well and truly gone.

Unless Ari could somehow come up with twenty dollars in the next fifteen minutes or so, he was sunk.

Rabbi Morgenstern woke that morning feeling strangely restless.

This was an unusual feeling for him. Normally, he was a cheerful man who enjoyed spending time with the boys in his fifth-grade classroom. He was a fine teacher and — because he instinctively knew what makes kids tick — he managed to maintain classroom discipline in a way that kept the atmosphere pleasant. All in all, as a rebbi he was a success.

Why, then, this feeling that he should be doing more?

After teaching the same subjects for five years in a row, he knew the material by heart and he knew how to present it to maximum effect. But Rabbi Morgenstern was beginning to feel that he needed to give his students something beyond the ordinary curriculum. Something that would help them not only become better students, but better, happier people.

What he needed, he decided as he put on his hat and jacket, was a challenge. Something that would stretch his wings, so to speak. But what?

Gershy was one of the first boys to reach their classroom that morning. Now he was busy doing what he'd been spending a lot of time doing in the month since he'd transferred to this school: pacing the halls.

He would prowl up one corridor and down the next, until about a minute before the bell rang. Then — he'd gotten his timing down to perfection — he'd slip back into the classroom and into his seat just before the rebbi walked in.

When the bell rang for lunch, he'd do the same thing. After gulping down his sandwich and bentching by himself, up and down the halls he went, until it was time to start afternoon classes. By now, Gershy had his system down to a science. He had it so that he could get through an entire day without exchanging a single word with his classmates.

Until this morning.

"Ouch!" Gershy looked up from the floor, where he'd gone sprawling when a two-ton missile crashed into him.

At a second glance, he realized that what he'd thought was a two-ton missile was really a kid in his class. Careening around a corner, Ari had collided with Gershy with the strength of a gale-force wind.

"S-sorry," Ari gasped. "I didn't see you."

"That's obvious," Gershy said, rubbing his sore elbow. He'd bumped it hard when he fell. "What's the big rush?"

"I have to go somewhere ...," Ari muttered.

"Where?" Gershy asked curiously. "Class'll be starting pretty soon."

"I'm not *going* to class."

"What? Why not?"

But Gershy was speaking to thin air. Ari had vanished.

•◎•◎•

It was the sound of thudding feet that told Gershy where the other boy had gone. He stared upwards, wearing a puzzled frown. Why was Ari in such a rush to go upstairs? There was nothing up there but the library ...

Driven by curiosity, he followed his classmate up the steps.

Gershy was extra careful to walk quietly, but Ari was so absorbed in his own thoughts that he probably wouldn't have heard a herd of elephants coming up behind him. He made straight for the library door and pushed it open.

The book-lined room was deserted at this hour of the day. Ari went to a small table and slumped into a chair. He had to think. He had to figure out what to tell his rebbi when he asked for the money.

It's only twenty dollars, he tried to tell himself. *I can ask my parents to lend it to me until I can figure out a way to pay it back ….*

But it wasn't so simple. For one thing, he'd given Rabbi Morgenstern his word that he'd have the complete sum by this morning. For another, if he told Rebbi how he'd come to lose the bill, he'd sound like such a fool ….

Which is exactly what I was, he thought gloomily. *What kind of dope counts money in the middle of a wind like that?*

He was startled by a sound. Someone was standing outside the library door, peeking in. Now that somebody was pushing open the door and walking in.

Ari sat up with a jerk. "Gershy! What are you doing here?"

Gershy strolled over to the table. It took every ounce of his willpower to hide his nervousness. What *was* he doing here?

"I could ask you the same thing," he drawled.

Ari flushed. "That's none of your business."

"Then you won't mind if I have a seat, right?" Gershy pulled out a chair and sat.

For a long, ludicrous moment, both boys stared off in different directions. The silence was deafening.

Finally, Ari burst out, "Why do you care, anyway? You aren't interested in any of us."

"Who says?" Gershy shot back, stung.

"Anyone who has eyes can see that you're totally uninterested in our class. Why else do you spend all your free time walking around by yourself instead of hanging around with other kids?"

"Maybe the 'other kids' aren't interested in hanging around with *me*!"

The minute the words were out of his mouth, Gershy regretted them. He stared down at the table, his face a dull, brick-red.

"What are you talking about?" Ari asked, momentarily diverted from his own troubles. "Sure we're interested!"

"Who says?" Gershy mumbled.

"*I* say! But you act like such a snob, walking around alone all the time, that no one thinks you even *want* them to be your friend!"

Gershy transferred his gaze from the tabletop to Ari. "I'm a snob?"

"Well, you sure act like one. Why don't you ever join in our games at recess? Or sit at our table during lunch?"

"I didn't think anyone wanted me there," Gershy admitted in a near-whisper. He'd only joined the fifth-grade class four weeks before, when his family had moved into the neighborhood.

"Well … you thought wrong."

Gershy felt his heart lift as though propelled upward by the wind. "Thanks," he said quickly. Then, to hide his emotions, he asked, "But why are you hiding up here? Is something wrong?"

Ari's face fell. "I'll say there's something wrong." In a few short, miserable sentences, he filled Gershy in on his problem.

"Uh-oh," Gershy said.

"You can ditto that," Ari said morosely. "Class starts in just ten minutes. And then … I'm sunk!"

Gershy nodded sympathetically. Ari gave him a small grin. His problem had not gone away — but at least now he wasn't looking at it alone.

Rabbi Morgenstern kissed his one-year-old good-bye, tickled his three-year-old, and smiled at his wife in farewell. Then he was out the door and on his way to yet another day in his fifth-grade classroom. Holding onto his hat in the vigorous wind, he went to his car and got behind the driver's wheel.

His strange mood lingered, but this was something he'd have to think about later. Right now, he had to concentrate on making the short drive to school, after which he'd face another day of transmitting important information and keeping a bunch of lively eleven-year-olds in check.

It didn't quite happen the way he'd envisioned it. There was a surprise waiting for Rabbi Morgenstern that morning.

He'd parked his car and was walking through the school gates when something caught his eye. A slip of dark-green paper was pressed against one of the slats of the fence, held in place by the force of the wind. Curious, the teacher reached for it and brought it close to his eyes.

No, he hadn't been mistaken. It was money. A twenty dollar bill!

Rabbi Morgenstern looked around. There was no one in sight on this windy morning. How had this money come to be here?

It could have come from anywhere, he reasoned. Why, someone a block away might have dropped this money — only to have it carried to this spot by the wind. There was simply no way of knowing whom the bill belonged to. With a shrug, Rabbi Morgenstern slipped it into his pocket. "Guess it's my lucky day," he murmured to himself.

He glanced at his watch. It was early. Maybe he'd go

to his favorite place, before class started, to think about the strange feeling he'd been entertaining all morning. He would try to figure out how he could be an even better rebbi. It was amazing what one could come up with if one was willing to bend the old noodle and give it some thought!

Hefting his briefcase, Rabbi Morgenstern started up the stairs.

•◎•◎•

The sound of footsteps sounded outside the library door. Both boys froze.

Rabbi Morgenstern pushed the door open — and opened his eyes wide in surprise.

"Hello, boys," he said, trying to mask his disappointment at finding the room occupied. "What brings you to the library so early in the morning?"

"Nothing," Gershy and Ari said in unison.

Looking more closely at their faces, he read traces of emotion and — in Ari's case — distress. The rebbi sank casually into the third chair at the table. "Is there a problem I can help with?"

"N-no problems, Rebbi," Ari stammered.

"Uh … actually," Gershy said bravely, with a sideways look at Ari, "there *is* something."

"I'm all ears." Rabbi Morgenstern settled more

comfortably into his seat, as though he had all day to listen.

Encouraged, Gershy spoke up again. "Ari's done a great job collecting money for our trip, Rebbi. The trouble is, the wind blew away a twenty dollar bill this morning — just as Ari was about to walk into the building. He doesn't know what to do."

There. It was out. Ari shot Gershy a look that was half-furious and half-grateful, and then waited tensely for his teacher's reaction.

Rabbi Morgenstern astonished them both by bursting into delighted laughter. "I think I can help with that." He reached into his pocket and pulled out — a twenty dollar bill!

"No, Rebbi. I can't take your money," Ari said at once. "This is my responsibility."

"And this is *your* money," Rabbi Morgenstern said with a smile. "I found it plastered to the school gate a few minutes ago."

He handed the bill to Ari, who received it with a dumbfounded look that quickly turned into a grin of vast relief. "Thanks, Rebbi!"

Rabbi Morgenstern turned to Gershy. "I understand why Ari was hiding up here. But what about you?"

"Gershy followed me," Ari volunteered. "He was curious to see where I was going."

"Really? Interesting," the rebbi said. "I've noticed, Gershy, that you usually spend most of your time on your own."

"That's because he thought no one was interested in being his friend," Ari said earnestly, ignoring the flush that was rising up from Gershy's collarbone. "But I told him he was wrong. *Dead* wrong!"

"Ari's absolutely right about that," the rebbi told Gershy seriously. "I don't think you've given your classmates a chance, Gershy. Or yourself ..."

Gershy sneaked a quick peek at Ari and seemed reassured by the look on the other boy's face. Rabbi Morgenstern glanced from one to the other. "Well," he said, "it looks like the wind blew in the solution to *two* problems this morning." He winked.

Ari and Gershy smiled bashfully.

"Why don't you go on back to class now, boys," their rebbi urged. "I'll be down in a few minutes." He still wanted to think over his own problem.

Suddenly, as the door closed behind his students, he had the first glimmering of an idea.

Maybe teaching was just one part of what he had a natural talent for doing. Maybe — just maybe — he was also cut out to help boys work through their problems — the way he'd done just now. To talk to them sincerely. And, even more important, to listen to them.

Maybe it was time to look into ways that he could relate to boys more personally than from simply behind a teacher's desk. The field was wide open. Wherever there were kids with problems, there was a need for someone to help ….

Rabbi Morgenstern looked up at the library ceiling, but his thoughts went far, far beyond it. "Thank You," he whispered.

It looked like the wind had blown in the solution to *three* problems that morning.

Feeling more excited than he'd felt in years, Rabbi Morgenstern went downstairs to his fifth-graders. The principal, passing him in the hall, remarked, "*You're* looking pretty happy this morning, Rabbi!"

"It's a great day, isn't it?" Rabbi Morgenstern beamed.

Walking into his classroom a minute later, he was gratified to see that at least two of his students' faces reflected the same joyous eagerness he was feeling. He grinned at Ari and Gershy, who grinned right back.

And class began.

Money in the Bank

I was just getting ready to call a friend and make plans for a lazy Sunday afternoon when the doorbell rang.

Curious, I went to answer it. In the doorway stood a woman I'd never seen before. She was carrying a baby girl in her arms, dressed in an adorable pink snowsuit. I'd never seen the baby before, either.

"I'm late," the woman said breathlessly. "The party's already started. Thanks so much, Faigy. Aviva's bottle is in the bag" — she handed me a bulging diaper bag — "along with some toys. There are some snacks in there, too; Aviva will eat pretty much anything. I'll be back at about four. Thanks so much!"

With that, she thrust the baby into my arms, leaned forward to kiss her chubby cheek, and disappeared down the path to her car.

I stood with my mouth open, watching her go. There were words waiting to spill out of my mouth, but somehow I couldn't say them. My head was spinning.

You know that game where you have to find the things that are wrong with a picture? There were quite a number of things wrong with this scenario.

For one thing, my name is not Faigy. It's Racheli. Faigy's my sister.

For another — who in the world was that woman,

and why had she just handed me her baby?

Slowly, I closed the door. Little Aviva gave me a gummy smile, which melted my heart.

"It looks like you're stuck with me until four," I told her. She gurgled and smiled some more.

I began to piece together the puzzle. My sister Faigy, who's exactly a year younger than I am, must have promised this woman to babysit her child today. (Though why she'd offered to do it at *our* house remained a mystery.) Somehow, Faigy had forgotten. She'd left the house nearly an hour ago; I hadn't a clue where. The woman had obviously mistaken me for her. Voila — instant babysitter!

I carried Aviva into the living room, where I divested her of the snowsuit. She kicked her feet with pleasure, clearly enjoying my company. At least I wasn't stuck looking after a baby who was terrified of strangers.

"I may not know who your mom is," I told her, "but I have a feeling that you and I are going to become good friends."

I'd just settled Aviva down on the carpet with the toys from her bag when the phone rang.

"Racheli!" It was my classmate, Michal. "Want to go ice skating with us? We'll be leaving in about fifteen minutes."

"Us" meant Michal's two sisters and her. One or

two other friends were probably part of the group, too, I surmised.

Sure enough, Michal chattered on, "Debby and Suri are coming over. Bring your skates!"

"Uh, I don't think I can make it." My heart was heavy. There's nothing I like better than ice skating. Under normal circumstances, I would have grabbed my skates and been on my way like a flash. Unfortunately, these were far from normal circumstances. "Thanks a bunch, Faigy," I muttered.

"What did you say?"

"Nothing, Michal. I'm sorry, I can't make it."

"Are you sure? We're going for ice cream afterwards. We'll have a ball!"

Heavily, I said, "I'm sure."

I hung up and sank down on the couch to feel sorry for myself.

"Racheli? Is anything wrong?" my mother asked, coming into the room with her coat on.

I looked up at her — just in time to see her spot the baby on the rug.

"Who's that?" she asked. Aviva smiled at her, and Ma smiled back.

"Her name's Aviva. That's all I know."

"Where did she come from?"

"A lady came to the door and practically threw her

at me. I think Faigy was supposed to babysit for her."

"Here?"

I shrugged. "Seems that way. Faigy must have forgotten."

Ma looked sympathetic. "So you're left holding the bag …."

"Right. Or rather — the baby. And Michal just called to invite me to go ice skating."

If the expression on my face hadn't told my mother exactly how I was feeling, the tone of my voice did. She sat down beside me. "Faigy went over to a friend's house. There's something going on there today, and she wanted to help. I'm not sure which friend, though. Do you want me to try to track her down and tell her to come home?" She paused. "Or maybe I could just babysit instead. It's not fair to have this job dumped on you."

"On you, either," I protested. "Besides, aren't you about to go out?"

"My errands can wait." She looked at me, waiting for me to make up my mind.

I'm only human. My first instinct was to grab at the chance to go ice skating. I'd never asked for this responsibility. Why should I have to carry it on this beautiful Sunday afternoon?

That was the crux of the problem: responsibility. As

the oldest of seven children, I have responsibility bred down deep in my bones. I may not have asked for Aviva today — but I had her. And I couldn't see myself giving that responsibility away so I could enjoy myself ice skating.

I tried. For about thirty seconds, I tried to talk myself out of that position.

"Don't be a martyr," I told myself. "Go out and have some fun with your friends! This is Faigy's problem, not yours."

Then, out of nowhere, I remembered an expression my *zeidy* always likes to use.

Zeidy is far away now and I hardly ever see him, but I still remember him very well. And I remember the things he taught me. When I was small and just learning about things like *mitzvos* and doing *chesed*, every time I did something good, my *zeidy* would say, "That's money in the bank!"

Finally, one day, I asked him what he meant.

"Up there," he said, pointing at the heavens, "there's a kind of 'bank' where all of us are collecting interest every day. Each time you do a mitzvah, you get a little richer up there. Every time you do a *chesed*, your 'bank account' grows a little larger. One day, Racheli, you'll be a very wealthy woman!"

I was facing a choice now. I could drag Faigy back

from whatever she was doing and be rid of a responsibility I'd never asked for.

Or I could decide to dump Aviva on my mother and fly away, carefree.

Or … I could put a little money in the bank.

I smiled at my mother. "Thanks anyway, Ma. I'm fine. I'll babysit for Aviva this afternoon. Isn't she adorable?"

By holding onto the edge of the couch, Aviva had managed to toddle her way over to where we were sitting. I scooped her up and tickled her. Aviva gave me a toothless giggle.

Maybe this job wouldn't be too bad after all.

That's what I thought at one p.m. By two-thirty, I was starting to change my mind.

Aviva had grown cranky, but she couldn't seem to fall asleep anywhere I put her down. I tried walking her around the house, hoping that she'd put her head on my shoulder and drop off. But the only thing that dropped was my heart, when she kept bursting into tears the minute I stopped walking.

Ma came back from running her errands. Her cheeks were pink from the fresh air, and she seemed relaxed and happy. I can't say I felt the same.

"How's it going, Racheli?" Ma asked as she took off her coat.

"It's going," I sighed. Aviva had perked up a bit at the sight of my mother. Ma held out her arms, and Aviva sagged into them.

"She's tired, poor thing," Ma crooned. "Why don't you put her down for a nap?"

"Believe me — I tried. She won't fall asleep."

That's when the phone rang. This time, it was my very best friend in the world. We'd been in the same class until last year, when she'd changed schools. Nevertheless, we were still as close as we'd ever been.

"Elisheva!" I exclaimed. "How are you?"

"Bored," she said. "Want to come over?"

I was tempted. Boy, was I tempted! Aviva was no longer the adorable creature that she'd been when I'd undertaken this job. My arms and feet and back were sore from tramping around the house with her. My mother was willing to babysit instead of me. Why not say "yes"?

But — Aviva was my responsibility. I hadn't asked for her; I'd never even agreed to take her. But sometimes responsibility is thrust on a person whether she likes it or not …

"No," I said slowly. "Or rather — yes, I'd love to. But I can't."

In a few succinct sentences, I outlined the state of affairs.

"Poor you!" Elisheva commiserated. "I'd come over there to keep you company, except that I'm supposed to be keeping an eye on the twins while my mother rests …. How about later? What time do you finish babysitting?"

"She said she'd be back around four."

"That's kind of late … unless you can stay for supper. I'll ask my mother when she wakes up."

We left it at that. My own mother wanted to start supper, so I took the baby back from her. The minute Aviva was in my arms she started wailing again.

Heaving a long sigh, I went back to my tramping. Aviva fell silent, for which I was thankful. But my back and my feet ached more than ever, and my heart was not far behind.

Mrs. Barron helped her friend, Mrs. Selinsky, put the final touch on the birthday cake and carry it out into the dining room, where two dozen or so twelve-year-olds were celebrating Aidel Selinsky's bas mitzvah. The girls burst into a hearty rendition of "Happy birthday to you," while the bas mitzvah girl's big sister, Mashi, and Mashi's friend served pieces of cake to each guest.

The girls were temporarily silent as they enjoyed their cake. Mrs. Barron used the opportunity to announce, "Your mothers will be here to pick you up in a few minutes, girls. I want to thank you all for coming, and for making this such an enjoyable party. Aidel and I would also like to thank my daughter Mashi, and Mashi's friend, Faigy Schwartzman, for helping us today."

Mrs. Barron rounded the table and came to a stop in front of Faigy. "You!" she exclaimed.

Faigy looked startled. "Excuse me?"

"*You're* Faigy Schwartzman?"

"That's right."

"Weren't you supposed to babysit for my Aviva today?"

Faigy's jaw dropped. "What?"

"I'm sure my sister-in-law said that she'd arranged it with you. I came to New York to stay with her and my brother this weekend so I could attend this bas mitzvah party. Mrs. Selinsky is one of my oldest friends ..." As Faigy continued to look thunderstruck, she added, "My sister-in-law lives on your block. Mrs. Edelman?"

Faigy blanched. "That was today?" She gulped. "I thought Mrs. Edelman said next Sunday ...."

The woman and the girl stared at each other. "If you're here," Mrs. Barron said, "then who did I give my daughter to?"

"Did she look like me? Near my age?"

Mrs. Barron nodded.

"That would be my sister, Racheli." Faigy rolled her eyes. "I think I'm in trouble …."

•◎•◎•

In the end, Aviva fell asleep about five minutes before her mother's car pulled up outside our house. I was watching at the window, so I saw her step out on the driver's side.

There was someone with her, coming out of the passenger side. To my amazement, that someone was my own sister, Faigy!

They reached the front door together. I was waiting for them.

"Racheli — I'm so sorry!" Faigy burst out as soon as she saw me.

"I seem to have given my baby to the wrong sister," Aviva's mother said dryly. "Hello, Racheli. My name is Mrs. Barron. Thank you for watching Aviva this afternoon."

"It was a pleasure, Mrs. Barron," I said, my head spinning. "But how did the two of you …?"

"We met at Aidel Selinsky's bas mitzvah party," Faigy told me. Her cheeks were crimson. "I *was* asked to watch Mrs. Edelman's guest's baby, but I guess I mixed up the dates …."

"I shouldn't have run away so quickly," Mrs. Barron said to me. "I didn't even give you a chance to tell me I'd gotten the wrong girl."

Mrs. Barron seemed as embarrassed as Faigy. Both of them stood before me as though I were a judge, about to render my verdict.

I could have shown resentment. After all, there was no question that I'd been taken advantage of. I'd missed out on two opportunities to have fun with my friends today, and had been burdened with looking after a child I'd never agreed to watch in the first place.

I could have stood in judgment on them, and made them feel even worse than they already did. But I didn't. I decided that I'd rather have money in the bank instead ….

"That's okay," I said cheerfully. "Aviva is the cutest thing. She's asleep now. She's right here …." I led Mrs. Barron to her sleeping child. While she was putting on Aviva's snowsuit, I turned to my sister. "Don't worry about it, Faigy. I didn't have any plans anyway."

Faigy gave me a grateful smile. Mrs. Barron gave me a nice bonus for all my trouble — on top of the usual babysitter's fee.

And my *zeidy* — though, admittedly, only in my mind — gave me a thumb's up, for remembering the most important lesson he'd ever taught me.

"Ma," I asked my mother later, "would you be able to deposit this for me?" I showed her Mrs. Barron's check.

She glanced at it. "That's a nice amount, Racheli. You certainly got paid well for your trouble."

"She'll be laughing all the way to the bank," Faigy remarked.

I hid a secret smile. My sister didn't know it, but she'd never spoken a truer word!

Brachi Comes Back

The Silmans were having a family meeting.

They didn't have these meetings often — only when something important was in the air. The six Silman kids (except for the baby, who was too young to understand what all the excitement was about) tumbled into the living room, eager to hear what was happening.

Rabbi and Mrs. Silman wasted no time telling them. "Cousin Brachi is coming," they said solemnly.

Gila, who was the oldest of the Silman kids and just about Brachi's age, opened her eyes wide. "Really?"

"Really," said Rabbi Silman. "Her older brothers will be going to camp, and her younger sisters will stay in the bungalow colony with Aunt Miriam this summer. But Brachi doesn't want to go to either one. She wants to come here."

This was flattering, Gila felt — but also a little scary. Would Brachi walk around crying all summer long? Would they have to tiptoe around her, afraid to laugh or fool around while she was so sad?

Mrs. Silman turned to her boys — five-year-old Shimi, and Yoni, who was only three. "Do you remember what I told you about Uncle Nosson?"

"You said he went to *shamayim*," said Shimi. Yoni didn't say anything.

"Yes," their mother said. "Uncle Nosson was very

sick, and then his *neshamah* went up to *shamayim*. That was in the winter. It's been a very sad time for Aunt Miriam and your cousins." She paused, looking around at all of her children. "So how are we going to treat Cousin Brachi when she comes?"

It was one of the twins who answered her. Shaindy and Shiri were nine years old and their memory of their cousin was dim. "We'll be nice to her, of course," Shaindy said. And Shiri added, "We'll try to cheer her up."

"Good!" Rabbi Silman boomed. "Remember, Brachi is coming here to get away from it all. It's been a heartbreaking year for her and her family. Let's all do our very best to give her a happy summer."

Gila left the meeting in a thoughtful mood. It was three whole years since she'd last laid eyes on Cousin Brachi. Three years ago, Uncle Nosson had still been healthy. The two families had spent Pesach together, here in California. Gila had some very happy memories of that time.

Still — three years was three years. A lot had happened in that time. Had her cousin changed very much? Would she and Brachi feel as close as before?

She had no way of knowing the answers to these questions. As her father would have put it: "Time will tell." And so, Gila sensibly put them out of her mind and went to call her friends to tell them the news: Cousin Brachi was coming!

Brachi felt her ears pop as the plane gained height. The sensation finally convinced her that this was real, and not some dream she was having in her own bed at home. She was really on a plane, on her way to her cousins in California! And, for the first time in her life, she was traveling on her own.

Of course, the airline had hung an "Unaccompanied Minor" sign around her neck, and there was a stewardess who was supposed to keep an eye out for her. But Brachi had said good-bye to her mother at the airport gate. The people seated on either side of her were strangers. For all intents and purposes, she was alone.

Usually, she didn't mind being alone. She'd been blessed with a lively imagination and had whiled away many a long, solitary walk making up interesting stories. But these days, her thoughts were the enemy. Every thought she had seemed to end up in the same place: the raw, hurting, empty space where her father had once been.

Each day, she woke up thinking she couldn't possibly miss him more — and each night, she went to bed knowing that she'd been wrong.

As the plane cut through the blue, blue sky and piles of unbelievably white clouds, Brachi thought about her father. Somehow, she felt closer to him at this height. As if *shamayim* was just on the other side of those clouds … A part of her wanted to stay on this plane forever, instead of down on solid ground, where all her pain would be waiting to greet her again.

When Ma had suggested this trip to California, Brachi had leaped at the idea. Maybe a completely different setting was just what she needed. Maybe her aunt and uncle and cousins would help her start viewing life as a cheerful thing again, and the world as a place where it was possible to be happy. Maybe.

She let her mind dwell on the family waiting for her at the other end of her journey.

There was Uncle Heshy, with his easy laugh and booming voice that could make any joke seem hilarious. Aunt Leah was warm and gentle — and a fantastic cook. Shaindy and Shiri had been six years old the last time Brachi had seen them. They'd adored her, following her around like twin shadows and hanging on to her every word. The memory made Brachi smile.

Little Shimi had been only two then, an adorable toddler. And Yoni, the baby, had spent hours and hours rocked in Brachi's willing arms.

There was a new baby now, she remembered. A

girl … what was her name again? Shani — that was it. Brachi looked forward to getting to know her, too.

In a world that had gone crazy this past year, it felt good to know that she was heading toward something utterly familiar. She knew her cousins the way she knew her own brothers and sisters. The plane sped on through the sky, moving inexorably westward.

For the first time since her father died, Brachi was actually looking forward to something.

The sign was slightly lopsided, but its message was colorful and warm:

WELCOME, BRACHI

To Your Home Away From Home!

But Brachi, exhausted from the trip and overwhelmed by all the new sights and sounds, hardly even saw it.

"The twins made the sign," her aunt said with a smile. Brachi returned a perfunctory smile of her own as she stared in dismay at the two boys capering around her. Was that big kid, playfully punching his brother in the arm, the adorable toddler she remembered? Shimi was five now, and he looked nothing like the child of Brachi's memory.

As for Yoni, he was unrecognizable from the sweet baby she'd held when she was last in this house. He stayed close to his brother, doing whatever Shimi did, laughing at his jokes and paying no attention at all to his cousin from New York.

The two boys whispered and giggled for a few minutes before Shimi pushed his younger brother toward Brachi. Yoni held out a bedraggled bunch of yellow wildflowers. Or were they weeds?

"They're for you," Shimi explained.

Brachi took them gingerly, with a startled, "Uh — thanks." A clump of soil dribbled off a stem and landed on Brachi's foot. When the boys weren't looking, she discreetly kicked it off.

She'd arrived just in time for supper. It was a strange meal. Brachi had to fight to keep her eyes open — but when she did open them, everyone looked different than she remembered.

Uncle Heshy had grown a beard. The twins, Shaindy and Shiri, did not gaze at her with delighted awe, as they had on her last visit when they were six. They were big fourth-graders now, chattering of this classmate and that teacher and some upcoming school trip. As soon as the meal was over, they disappeared upstairs to call their friends.

Shimi told a lot of jokes — none of them, in Brachi's

opinion, very funny. But Uncle Heshy told hardly any jokes at all. He was more serious than she remembered. She'd expected him to be the same rollicking uncle she remembered. Instead, he smiled gently at her and asked if she wanted seconds. Soon afterwards he stood up, saying that he had to go prepare.

"Abba gives a *shiur* now," Gila told her cousin. "At the shul, every night after Ma'ariv."

Brachi nodded, impressed and confused at the same time. Where was the Uncle Heshy she knew?

"Do you like the chicken?" Aunt Leah asked, smiling at Brachi across the table. "I remembered that it was your favorite."

"It's delicious," Brachi said automatically. Actually, it tasted like sand in her mouth. She wasn't very hungry.

She would have loved to have a quiet chat with Aunt Leah, as she'd often done with such pleasure on their last visit together. But Aunt Leah had a new baby now. Shani was just four months old and *very* cranky. It seemed to Brachi that Shani never stopped crying.

Aunt Leah looked more tired than Brachi remembered. Rather than spend any length of time talking to her niece from New York, she vanished upstairs to nurse and soothe the baby. Shimi and Yoni also went upstairs, to play some mysterious game of their own in their room until bedtime.

Which left Gila.

The two girls changed into their pajamas and climbed into the twin beds in Gila's room. Brachi had enjoyed many a long, confidential talk with her cousin on her previous visit. Back then, Gila had been nine years old and struggling to make friends.

Tonight, she talked of nothing *but* her friends. Gila seemed to have become Miss Popularity in the years they'd been apart.

Somewhere in the middle of her cousin's monologue, Brachi fell asleep.

The next day, Brachi was a lot more alert than she'd been the night before. In a way, that was worse. Now she was really aware of all the changes.

The aunt and uncle and cousins she'd expected to see seemed to have disappeared — to be replaced by a whole different set of relatives. An Uncle Heshy who gave *shiurim* instead of telling jokes; a weary Aunt Leah who spent all her time feeding or rocking a testy infant; a Shaindy and Shiri who were far too busy with their own friends to spare more than a passing thought for their New York cousin; a Shimi who was a pesky kid instead of a cute, huggable toddler. And a Yoni who was simply — unrecognizable.

Even the new baby, Shani, twisted up her face and started wailing when Brachi tried to pick her up. Disappointment flooded her like an ocean at high tide. The disappointment soon gave way to anger, and a kind of grief. She'd lost so much this year. She didn't want to lose anything else. Not — one — more — thing!

But it was the change in Gila that hurt the most. Gila, who'd been her closest cousin. They'd shared secrets, reveling in the knowledge that they were friends *and* relatives at the same time. Now Gila had grown up. She was already a bas mitzvah and didn't need Brachi in the same way anymore. It was all different now ....

There came a point in the middle of that first full day in California when Brachi couldn't bear it for even one more minute. Slipping away to the stairs, she began to climb. And climb. Up, up, up she went, to where there weren't any more stairs left to climb.

She left the painful world behind and climbed higher and higher, almost as high as she'd been on the plane, to the uppermost point in the house. Then she pushed the trapdoor open and entered the attic.

She sneezed. The place was dusty, with its cardboard boxes and broken furniture and old clothes and abandoned toys. She and Gila used to play dress-up here and cut out paper dolls. But those things, too, belonged to the past.

Thinking of the past, and of all the things that

would never be the same, Brachi drew her knees up to her chin, put her head down on them, and sobbed as if her heart was breaking all over again.

•◎•◎•

It was Gila who noticed that Brachi was missing.

She considered telling her mother, but Ma was feeding the baby, and anyway, Gila didn't want to worry her. Where could her cousin have gone?

She began to search the house.

She checked the basement and first floor, and was about to start on the bedrooms — when she remembered the attic. Quick as a wink, she darted up the stairs. Up and up … She pushed open the trapdoor and poked her head through.

The first thing she saw was a huddled figure, gazing through the smudged window that looked out over the yard.

"There you are!" Gila cried with relief. She came in, letting the door fall shut behind her. "Why'd you come up here all by yourself, Brachi?" Now that she was closer, she could see the telltale pinkness around her cousin's eyes. Brachi had been crying.

At first, it seemed as if Brachi wouldn't answer at all. Then the words came. They seemed to bubble up from some deep place inside, rising with explosive force until they burst uncontrollably forth.

"Everything's so different!" Brachi wailed.

Gila looked blank. "What do you mean? What's different?"

"You are! All of you."

"Well, that's natural, isn't it? We're all three years older. You've grown up, too."

"But I don't *want* things to change," Brachi sniffled. In a near-whisper, she added, "I need them to be the same. That's what I was looking forward to …."

Gila looked sad. "I'm sorry."

"It's not your fault," Brachi almost snapped. "But I hate it. It's not what I expected."

For some reason, this made Gila mad. "Is that *our* fault?"

"Fault, shmault." Brachi shrugged unhappily. "I hate it, that's all."

"Well, thanks a lot," Gila said huffily. "After everything we did to make you feel welcome."

Now it was Brachi's turn to look surprised. "Like what?"

"I suppose you didn't notice the sign the twins made for you. They worked two whole evenings on that thing!"

Brachi was abashed. To tell the truth, she *hadn't* really noticed.

"And the flowers that Shimi and Yoni picked for

you. They worked hard on that, too. And no one even made them do it!"

Brachi remembered only a clump of mud falling on her shoe.

"And Ma cooked your favorite supper. But you didn't even notice …"

Brachi looked down.

"And *I*," Gila continued inexorably, "was planning to invite my friends over on Shabbos, especially to meet you. But only if you'll bother to notice *them*!"

Brachi looked at her cousin. "I'm sorry."

"You're sorry?" Gila yelped. "*You're* sorry?"

For some reason, this struck both girls as hysterical. They started laughing, and once they started they couldn't stop. They laughed until their sides ached and tears ran from their eyes. Then a silence fell. It was mostly a comfortable silence, though for Gila it was also a waiting one. She fixed her eyes on her cousin. Brachi looked out the window. The sky was darkening toward dusk. Her first full day in California was drawing to an end. She hadn't found the comfort and the freedom from sadness that she'd hoped for as she'd winged her way across the country to reach this place.

But she had found something else.

She'd found the family she loved — a little older, a little wiser and certainly a little different. They weren't the people she was expecting … but then, she didn't think *they'd* got what they were expecting, either. And there was not a thing that any of them could do about that but accept each other, just the way they were.

She felt the old, familiar sadness well up inside. She'd come here hoping her aunt and uncle and cousins could make her happy again. But maybe happiness wasn't a gift they could give her, wrapped up in pretty paper and ribbons. Maybe it was something she had to find for herself, no matter how long it took ….

The sky held another message for her, as well: You can't depend on people to stay the same. In a world where change can happen with horrifying swiftness, or slowly over the course of years, there was only one thing that she could count on *not* to change.

She looked up again, but this time she wasn't looking for her father. She was looking for her Father — because He was the only constant. He would never go away or leave her alone. He would never change.

"Ready to go down now?" Gila asked softly. She'd grown tired of waiting for Brachi to say something.

Brachi turned. To Gila's relief, her eyes weren't filled with tears. While she didn't look exactly happy, she looked peaceful.

"Yes," she said. "I think I'm ready now."

And they went downstairs together.

Taking It Slow

It was one of those brisk, windy days in October that make you feel like singing out loud. I compromised by humming under my breath as I walked to school. A smile was more or less permanently glued to my face throughout the morning.

Lunchtime still found me in the highest of spirits, even though Hadassah, a classmate of mine, managed to trip over her own feet and spill the contents of her lunch bag all over my uniform skirt.

"Oh! I'm sorry," Hadassah blurted. Her cheeks had gone very red and her eyes wide with a hint of dampness.

"It's okay," I said, brushing her apologies away along with the tuna fish on my skirt.

"But I'm *really* sorry," Hadassah said earnestly.

"I know. And it's *really* okay!" With that, I turned away and hurried over to join my friends, who were already hard at work on their own lunches. What did a slightly fishy-smelling skirt matter on such a glorious day?

Besides, it had been my own fault. I should have known better than to stand anywhere near Hadassah in the lunchroom. Hadassah is … I guess the best word for it is *slow*. She's also kind of clumsy, with a sweet, shy smile that seems to beg the world not to be mad at her. She manages to keep up with our class … barely. Even her name is slow. Whereas any of us would have shortened it to "Dassi," Hadassah's name takes all of three syllables to pronounce!

"Hi, Chani! What kept you so long?" My friend Sara waved a sandwich in welcome.

"A slight accident," I said briefly. I was in no mood to discuss it. Outside the tall windows, leaves were skittering back and forth in a light, joyous dance. My heart felt just as light.

The main reason I was so thrilled about the weather was because we were scheduled to take a "nature trip" with our Science teacher, Miss Glibman, that afternoon. We couldn't have had a more perfect day for it. Miss Glibman had instructed us to bring along a new, hardcover notebook, which we were going to use for a special nature project. I couldn't wait.

I was halfway through my lunch when, from the corner of my eye, I saw Hadassah make her laborious way across the big room clutching a brown paper bag. It had taken her all this time to collect the scattered pieces of her lunch. It would take her nearly as long to find an empty spot at one of the tables. By the time she actually started eating, the bell would have rung and the rest of us would be stampeding out the door. Poor Hadassah. She was never quite in sync with the rest of us …

All too soon, the bell rang. An invisible hand seemed to sweep us all toward the big double doors. I glanced over my shoulder as I passed through.

In the vast, empty room, Hadassah was the only one still seated at one of the long tables, slowly packing up the remains of her unfinished lunch.

•◎•◎•

"Did everyone remember to bring a hardcover notebook?" Miss Glibman asked from the front of the room. "Raise your hand if you have one."

All across the room, hands shot up like weeds in the summer. Only one hand remained unraised.

"Hadassah?"

Hadassah's eyes welled with tears. "I'm sorry, Miss Glibman," she almost whispered. "I forgot."

"I told you to write it down in your assignment book," the teacher snapped.

"I know. But I l-left my assignment book in school …."

The sigh that Miss Glibman heaved was audible down to the back row. "Luckily, I brought a couple of extra notebooks — just in case." Poor Hadassah always seemed to fall into that category. Just in case …

"Okay," Miss Glibman said. "The bus is waiting outside. Line up, girls."

There was an eager bustle as we stood up, retrieved

our backpacks from the back of the room and headed for the exit. The buses would be bringing us back just in time for dismissal.

Once again, I looked over my shoulder. Hadassah was struggling to zip up her knapsack. The room emptied, leaving her alone. With rising impatience I watched her fumble with the zipper, while outside the bus waited and my friends tumbled laughing out the door.

I was about to urge her to hurry when the words were taken right out of my mouth.

"Hurry up, Hadassah," Miss Glibman urged. "We want to have plenty of time at the nature reserve this afternoon."

Hadassah looked up, nodded agreeably and bent over the stubborn zipper again.

With a sigh, Miss Glibman went over to help her.

The bus ride passed as all such rides do, in song and chatter and lots of laughter. We reached the nature reserve in about forty-five minutes. As we pulled into the parking lot, the talk died down for a moment. I guess we lost our breaths for a second — the scenery was that breathtaking.

Autumn foliage dazzled the eye with brilliant crimsons, oranges and yellows. On the ground, the scattered leaves refused to lie still; they pranced and leaped about with every gust of the wind. I stepped off the bus with the others and filled my lungs with clear, crisp air. We'd left our backpacks on the bus, but each of us held a notebook in our hands. Hadassah, I saw, was holding one, too.

"Now," Miss Glibman said as we surrounded her in a large, ragged circle, "here's what I want you to do, girls. As you can see, there are a few moderately pretty leaves around here …." She waited for the laughter to die down. "I want you to pick up the prettiest leaves you can find and place each one between two pages of your notebook. We're going to make pressed-leaf albums!"

There was an excited murmur. Some girls started inching away toward the trees, eager to get started. Miss Glibman told us a few more things about how to press the leaves and when to meet back at the bus. Then, at her signal — we were off!

Sara and I started out together, but we soon lost sight of one another as each of us followed the leaves that caught our eye. I was soon wandering among some trees, contentedly picking leaves and then discarding them when a better one came along. Each leaf was more beautiful than the one before. My notebook began to fill with dry, crackling color. I was reaching for a particularly stunning specimen when, through the trees, I spied Hadassah.

She was sitting quite still at the foot of a tall tree, examining a leaf that she held in her hand. Over and over she turned the leaf, studying every line and tint in her slow, intent way. She seemed to be savoring that leaf. She certainly wasn't thinking of the next one. Only one single leaf existed in the universe for Hadassah at that moment ….

I felt a pang. I'd thought *I* was seeing the beauty of the leaves, but compared to Hadassah I hadn't even started. What did she know that I didn't?

Hidden by a broad tree trunk, I watched her for a minute. At this rate, Hadassah would never fill her notebook. I pictured what would happen when we returned to the bus and showed Miss Glibman our work. All of us would proudly hold up our bulging notebooks. Hadassah would hang her head and show her one perfect leaf.

I thought about what it must be like to be Hadassah. To move through the world in slow motion, like a toddler just learning to walk and stopping to gaze in wonder at everything around him. Hadassah had that same, childlike quality. She would probably enjoy the leaves more than any of us — but finish her project on time? Not a chance!

The sad thing was this: *She* would be the one to appreciate nature, but *we* would be the ones to get high marks on our nature project ….

That, I decided, was just not fair.

On impulse, I took the largest and most finely-colored leaf from my notebook and held it carefully in my hand as I began to slip through the trees. I came up behind Hadassah, who was still poring over her leaf like a mother over her beloved baby. The noise of the wind rustling in the trees covered any sound I made. Moving very slowly, I reached over from behind and let my leaf flutter down onto Hadassah's notebook.

Startled, she picked it up. I melted back into the trees and hid again, watching. Hadassah had plucked my leaf from her notebook and was gazing at it with an expression of rapture. After a while, she opened the notebook and placed first her own leaf, and then mine, between its pages.

It had worked! It occurred to me that if I could do it once, I could do it again. I could keep putting leaves where Hadassah would be sure to find them …. I was hurrying now, eyes down to find leaves not only for myself, but for Hadassah, too.

With my eyes focused on the ground, I had no idea that someone was coming toward me until I walked right into her.

"Oof!" I clutched my stomach and looked up. "M-Miss Glibman!"

My teacher was as surprised as I was. Reaching up to pat down her hair, which had become disarranged in the collision, she asked, "Chani, have you seen Hadassah, by any chance?"

"Uh, yes. She's over that way." I pointed.

Miss Glibman nodded her thanks and hurried on. Curious, I followed. I went discreetly, trying not to rustle the leaves too much as I walked. Hadassah was right where I'd left her.

"Hello, Hadassah," Miss Glibman said.

"H-hi, Miss Glibman." Hadassah looked up nervously.

"How's it going?"

"Okay. I have two leaves so far."

I could imagine Miss Glibman stifling a sigh. The rest of the class must have nearly filled their notebooks by this time.

"Oh, look!" the teacher exclaimed suddenly. "There's a really nice one. And there's another one! Why don't you take them, Hadassah?"

Hadassah leaned down to pick up the leaves Miss Glibman had pointed to. As she did, Miss Glibman quickly deposited two more leaves on top of Hadassah's notebook.

"Good luck!" the teacher sang out cheerily. She turned and came back the way she'd come — directly toward me. I held my breath.

Miss Glibman had nearly passed me when I heard her murmur under her breath, "Doing a little spying, Chani?"

I jumped six inches. Blushing furiously, I stepped out from behind my tree. "I was just — uh — just …"

She eyed me closely. "Just what?"

I let out my breath all at once. "Just doing what you did, Miss Glibman."

For a second, she stared at me in surprise. Then, slowly, her face relaxed into a smile.

"Oh? With what success?"

"I managed to give her one nice, big leaf. She already had one of her own." We were whispering.

"Well, I just gave her four!" Miss Glibman whispered with a broad smile.

"I know," I said with a grin. "I saw you."

She motioned for me to walk with her. As we put some distance between ourselves and Hadassah, we resumed our ordinary voices.

"I felt badly about the way I'd snapped at Hadassah in class earlier," Miss Glibman said matter-of-factly. "Sometimes I'm too impatient with her."

"Uh, me, too," I said, a little awkwardly.

She threw me a sideways glance. “Does it surprise you that a teacher can feel impatient?”

I shook my head. “Not really. It just surprises me that …”

“That I can admit it?”

I nodded bashfully.

“Teachers are human, too,” Miss Glibman told me. “We’re always supposed to be working on our *middos* — just like our students. It’s a process that takes a lifetime, you know.”

I nodded again. I was temporarily tongue-tied — an unusual situation for me.

“Hadassah has something to teach all of us,” my teacher said as we strode through the trees. “If ever there was someone who moved patiently and thoughtfully through life, it’s her.”

“I know,” I said. And I meant it.

We trudged along in silence for a few more minutes, thinking about Hadassah. Then Miss Glibman said, “Come on. We’d better get back to the bus. It’s almost time.”

As we hurried along, my teacher asked, “So, did you enjoy the outing?”

For the third time, I nodded. “I feel like I … accomplished a lot.”

“Good!” She smiled.

I broke out in a smile of my own as Hadassah came ambling through the trees some time later — naturally, the last one to arrive. But she held her notebook in both hands as though it were a precious prize. I could tell that she was feeling pretty accomplished, too.

I remembered the way she'd gazed and gazed at that one precious leaf. It seemed to put a whole new spin on things.

Taking things slow … *Hmm.* Could Hadassah know something that I don't?

A Member of the Family

Lani was a walker. While other girls her age might balk moving from point A to point B with nothing but their own two feet for locomotion, Lani never complained. In fact, she relished a good, long walk.

Now that spring was here and the days were longer, she often took a walk around the neighborhood after school. She enjoyed seeing the little kids out with their balls and jump ropes, and checking on the progress of the newly-blossomed flowers. Usually, she was back in plenty of time to wash up and join the family at the supper table.

One day, however, her father noticed an empty chair.

"Where's Lani?" he asked, as his wife set down the big tureen and started ladling out bowls of piping-hot bean soup.

"I don't know," she answered with a slight frown. "She went out for a walk a while ago and hasn't come back yet."

At that moment, Lani's two little sisters started squabbling over whose turn it was to sit next to Daddy, which distracted Lani's mother for a minute. As soon as she'd settled the problem, she turned back to her husband. "I don't like this. It'll be dark soon."

"Neither do I. If Lani can't be responsible, we may have to restrict her outings."

"Is Lani getting punished?" Shabsi, Lani's younger brother, asked with interest.

"That's none of your business," Lani's older sister, Chevi, retorted.

"I asked Daddy, not you!" Shabsi looked at his father. "Is she?"

"I don't believe that's any concern of yours, Shabsi," Daddy replied. But there was a furrow between his eyes that did not bode well for Lani.

They were finished with the soup and in the middle of the main course when the phone rang. Shabsi pounced on it. "Hello?"

A second later, his expression changed. "Lani! Boy, are you in trouble ...."

"I'll take that," his mother said, holding out her hand. With a sheepish grin, Shabsi handed her the phone. She listened in silence for a few minutes before hanging up.

"Lani will be home in a few minutes," Ma said, turning back to the table.

"Where is she?" Daddy asked.

Ma looked puzzled. "Apparently, at some elderly woman's house. A Mrs. Hirschman, she said. Over on Central Street."

"Mrs. Hirschman?" Now he looked just as puzzled as she did.

"Yes. How she ended up there, I haven't a clue. I guess we'll have to wait till she gets home to hear the whole story."

Lani's little sisters chose that moment to start fighting, which effectively wiped all thoughts of the errant Lani from everyone's mind for a while.

But only for a while. As soon as the front door opened, Lani was front and center again.

She came in looking guilty and happy at the same time. "Hi, everyone! Sorry I'm late …."

"So are we," her father said dryly. "Go wash up, and sit down to eat something. We can't wait to hear your story."

Trying not to talk with her mouth full, Lani was soon telling her rapt family about the tumble she'd taken right in front of a weather-beaten house surrounded by a sagging picket fence. "There I was, just walking along and minding my own business, when this kid on a bike rode right into me!"

"Are you okay?" Ma asked worriedly. "Did you hurt yourself?"

"Just scraped my knees. No big deal … Anyway, my knees were smarting pretty bad. I wanted to clean up the blood, and I wasn't sure if I'd be able to walk home right away. Just then, the door of the house opened and this lady came out."

"Which lady?" Shabsi asked.

"The lady I'm telling you about. Mrs. Hirschman. She's pretty old, but let me tell you, she can move pretty fast. She practically ran out of the house to ask me if I was okay. She'd seen me through the window."

"That was nice of her," Chevi commented. "What did you do?"

"Mrs. Hirschman insisted that I come inside and do something for my knees, and also rest up a little before going home. I felt like I wouldn't mind sitting down for a minute, so I said okay and went in."

Lani took some time to eat some more, while her family waited impatiently. Finally, Shabsi said, "And then?"

"And then," Lani said, putting down her fork, "Mrs. Hirschman got me band-aids for my scrapes — after I'd washed them and sprayed them with that antibiotic stuff — and a drink of water. She made me say my *brachah* out loud so she could say '*Amein*' .... Then we talked for a while."

"About what?" Chevi asked, fascinated.

Lani shrugged. "All kinds of things. My school, and my family, and her house, which she told me is nearly a hundred years old! And it looks it, too ..."

"Does she have a husband?" Ma asked.

"She had one. She showed me his picture. He looks

like a real tzaddik! But he's not alive anymore. Mrs. Hirschman looked sad when she told me about him. He was a rebbi in a yeshivah, she said. He was *niftar* ten years ago, but I think she still misses him a lot."

"I'm sure she does," her father said quietly. Lani's mother looked thoughtful.

Suddenly, Lani remembered something. "Mrs. Hirschman gave me a present for you, Ma."

Her mother looked surprised. "For me?"

Lani nodded. "Something homemade — strudel, I think she called it. She felt bad about my being late for supper. I left the bag by the front door when I came in."

Shabsi was sent to the front door to fetch the bag. In short order he returned, bearing a tidy, foil-wrapped package.

"*I* want some!" Lani's little sister crowed, as soon as she laid eyes on the pastry.

"Me, too!" her even younger sister demanded.

"We'll all have a piece," Ma said. "Chevi, please get me a sharp knife …."

The strudel was delicious. The unknown Mrs. Hirschman was praised for her baking abilities, as well as her kindness to Lani.

"You should call her tomorrow and thank her again," Daddy suggested to Lani.

"I'm going to do better than that. I'm going to visit her. She said I could. I think," Lani said, "she's a little lonely."

The next afternoon, when Lani came home from school, she found a package waiting beside her snack on the kitchen table.

"What's this?" she asked.

"A present for Mrs. Hirschman — some of my homemade brownies. I put a note inside, too, thanking her for yesterday."

"Great!" No doubt Lani was hoping for a taste of those brownies when she gave them to Mrs. Hirschman. Ma quickly put an end to those dreams with a firm, "No cake before supper, Lani!"

"Okay," she said with some reluctance. Did that, she wondered, include cookies? She'd seen a nice cookie jar on Mrs. Hirschman's counter. And roller-blading sure helped her work up an appetite …

Lani's second visit with Mrs. Hirschman was a roaring success. She came home with her head full of the stories Mrs. Hirschman had told her from her long and interesting life — and her hands full of the peanut-butter cookies that Mrs. Hirschman had sent over.

"You should go visit her *every* day, Lani," Shabsi urged, cookie crumbs ringing his lips. "These are good!"

"They sure are," Lani agreed. "Mrs. Hirschman knows some great riddles, too. She asked me some really funny ones today. And then she asked if *I* know any jokes or riddles."

"Yay! Someone else to listen to Lani's jokes," Shabsi cheered. "That lets us off the hook. You *should* go see her more often, Lani."

"I will," Lani assured him loftily. "For your information, Mrs. Hirschman thought my jokes were great."

"I guess there's no accounting for tastes ...."

"I'm going to send you back tomorrow with some of my lemon squares," Ma planned.

Daddy smiled. "You two ladies seem to be becoming like pen-pals. Culinary pen-pals ..."

Ma turned to him, eyes alight. "You're right. Why should we keep sending food and messages back and forth? Let's invite her here for a Shabbos meal!"

Lani thought that was a great idea. "Except," she said doubtfully, "it'll be kind of a long walk for Mrs. Hirschman."

"Then we'll have her for the whole Shabbos. I'm going to look up her number and call her tomorrow," her mother decided.

And that's what she did. Mrs. Hirschman was a little flustered by the unexpected invitation, but very pleased to accept it. Lani's father drove by to pick her up on Friday afternoon, to save her the trouble of taking the bus.

The whole family soon found themselves warming to their guest. Mrs. Hirshman looked like everybody's favorite *bubby*. Her smile was warm, her attention span for dumb jokes endless, and her homemade apple pie — which she'd brought for dessert — simply out of this world!

"I can see that you're going to become a frequent guest in this house," Lani's father said with a smile, as the whole family clustered around to say good-bye to Mrs. Hirschman before he drove her home after Shabbos. "You've made a real hit with the kids."

"Thank you." The old woman's eyes glowed. "I haven't had this much fun in a long time."

"Come again soon," Ma urged. And her children seconded that motion in no uncertain terms.

So it was no surprise when Mrs. Hirschman accepted an invitation to spend another Shabbos, just two weeks later. This time, she came with a bottle of sparkling grape juice and a home-baked banana cream pie. Shabsi eyed the pie longingly. Dessert seemed such a long way off ….

"Tell me, Mrs. Hirschman," Ma asked on Friday night, over the chicken soup. "Do you have any children?"

Two splotches of pink appeared on Mrs. Hirschman's cheeks. "I wish you could meet them!" she exclaimed. "Binyamin and Sara. Unfortunately, they both live far away from here."

"Where?" Daddy asked with interest.

"Binyamin lives in Detroit. And Sara lives …" She choked a little over her soup, and spent a few seconds coughing before she lifted her face, pinker than ever. "What a scatterbrain I've become in my old age! To think that a mother could forget where her own daughter lives … Miami! That's it. She's in Miami, and very happy there."

"Any *eineklach*?" Ma asked politely.

"Six! I've got six of them. And eleven great-grandchildren, too, *bli ayin hara*. Such *zeeskeit*s, all of them …"

"Do you have any pictures?"

"Oh, no — not here. Maybe I'll bring them another time …."

But the next time she came, there were no pictures. "Me and my scatterbrain!" she exclaimed ruefully. "Can I offer this instead?"

"This" turned out to be a dozen homemade cream puffs. It was a quite acceptable substitute for pictures of her grandchildren, Lani and her siblings thought.

Mrs. Hirschman soon became a regular Shabbos

guest at their home. She played long board games with the older kids, read the little ones bedtime stories, and chatted pleasantly with the parents. When she went back to her weather-beaten, century-old house, they were always sorry to see her go.

"Guess what?" Ma said as she greeted Lani after school one day. "I ran into an old friend in the supermarket this morning. She lives in Detroit now and is here visiting family. I asked her if she happens to know anyone named Hirschman in Detroit — and she does. He's a doctor in their community. I wonder if he's our Mrs. Hirschman's son?"

"She never said he was a doctor," Lani remarked.

"I know. But then again, she didn't tell us very much about him at all — or her daughter. I think I'll give her a call and ask. Just out of curiosity ..." In two strides, Ma was at the phone.

Lani, busy eating a muffin while reading a book, soon lost track of the conversation. It was the silence afterwards that caught her attention.

She looked up. His mother was sitting opposite her, looking troubled.

"What's the matter, Ma? Is Mrs. Hirschman okay?"

"She seemed fine — at first," Ma said slowly. "It was

after I mentioned that Dr. Hirschman in Detroit that she started acting … funny."

"Funny? How?"

"I'm not sure. She sort of clammed up. Would hardly say a thing, except, 'No, that doctor is not my son.' Then she found an excuse to hang up quickly."

"Did you invite her for Shabbos?" Lani asked.

"I never got the chance. She hung up so fast …."

The next day, Ma tried again. It was already Wednesday — time to make Shabbos plans.

But Mrs. Hirschman was not coming for Shabbos. She had other plans, she told Ma. Thank you very much, anyway, though ….

She said the same thing the following week. *And* the week after that …

"Something's wrong," Ma told Lani on Sunday.

"I know," Lani said miserably. "I tried going over to visit her three times already. Each time, she made some excuse for not inviting me inside."

"Daddy and I think that maybe we've done something to offend her. Can you think of anything?"

Lani shook her head, the picture of gloom.

Ma mused out loud. "Mrs. Hirschman lives all by herself. Until a few weeks ago, she seemed very happy to be with us. Now she's had a dramatic change of heart. What I want to know is — why?"

Abruptly, she stood up. "Come on, Lani."

"Where are we going?" She scrambled to her feet.

"To solve the mystery, once and for all."

They were silent on the short drive over to Mrs. Hirschman's house. Ma looked at the narrow gray house, with its peeling paint and sagging fence. She felt a pang. Why would their new friend suddenly turn her back on them? Had they done something to hurt her feelings?

She led the way up the weed-strewn path, with Lani following close behind. But when they got to the door, she stood aside. "You knock," she whispered. "She's used to seeing *you* at her door …."

Lani's knock was answered after a fairly lengthy interval, as though Mrs. Hirschman had been reluctant to answer. Her face creased into a smile when she saw who it was.

"Lani! How are you doing?"

"I'm fine, *baruch Hashem*, Mrs. Hirschman. I — I brought my mother with me today." She gestured at Ma, whom Mrs. Hirschman had not noticed till now.

Something in Mrs. Hirschman's face seemed to close down. It was as if someone had just slammed a shutter over a window to keep out the bad weather. The old woman retreated a step.

"Please," Ma said, moving closer. "Don't shut me

out. I came because I must have done something to hurt you, and I need to know what it was. So that I can say 'I'm sorry,' and ask you to forgive me …"

The invisible shutter flew open. Mrs. Hirschman stared at Ma. "There's nothing to forgive! Is that what you've been thinking … all this time?"

Silently, Ma nodded.

Slowly — to Lani's horror — Mrs. Hirschman's eyes filled. "I'm the one who's sorry," she whispered. "I have to ask you to forgive *me* …."

"It all started when I called you that day," Ma said. "When I asked you if the Dr. Hirschman in Detroit is your son. You told me that he's not. So, what …?" Suddenly, she broke off, as understanding dawned. "Mrs. Hirschman? Do you *have* a son?"

The old woman shook her head. The tears were falling openly now, but she made no move to wipe them away. "No … I don't have any children."

"B-but —" Lani couldn't restrain herself. "Binyamin … Sara … all those adorable great-grandchildren … They don't even *exist*?"

"No … I'm sorry. I told you — all of you — a lie. It was very wrong of me." Her voice shook.

"But — *why*?"

"I think I know why," Ma said softly. She looked at Mrs. Hirschman. "It made you feel a little better, didn't it? Living here all alone, you must feel very lonely at times. And then you met us, and we didn't know anything about you. So you made up the kind of life you wish you'd had, with children and grandchildren to love you and give you *nachas* … Am I right?"

Mrs. Hirschman bobbed her head. She was crying into her hands.

Lani stepped forward and gazed earnestly at the old woman. "Don't cry, Mrs. Hirschman," she begged. "Don't feel bad. We all pretend sometimes. My brother Shabsi pretends that there are two big cops standing outside our door at night, because he's afraid of the dark!"

Mrs. Hirschman lowered her hands, and there was the glimmer of a smile shining through the tears. "Does he?"

"Sure! And sometimes *I* make things up, too — just to make myself feel better. Like pretending I aced a test, when I really know I did lousy. We're not mad at you for making up that stuff about your kids. Not a bit!"

"Thank you, Lani," Mrs. Hirschman said quietly. She rubbed her damp cheeks.

"Besides," Ma said, taking the old woman's hand, "there's no need to make up stories anymore. Because you *have* a family now."

Mrs. Hirschman's eyes widened. "I do?"

"Of course you do! Did you think a few weeks away were going to make my kids forget their favorite *bubby*?"

For a minute, Mrs. Hirschman looked as if she didn't know whether to break into the world's biggest smile, or burst into tears again.

It was close … but the smile won.

"Why are we standing on the doorstep?" she asked, in an entirely different tone of voice. "I've got some homemade butterscotch bars just waiting for someone to taste them!"

As she ushered her newfound "family" inside, even the sagging gray house seemed to straighten up and stand at attention. Weather-beaten or not, there was life inside those old walls yet!

And even better — there was love.

Going in Circles

It was snowing — a big, beautiful snowstorm that made everyone happy. Everyone but me.

It's not that I don't love snow. I do. The sight of all those swirling, whirling flakes was just as pretty as ever, and normally I would have been right beside my younger sisters and brother at the front window, drinking it all in.

But the snow didn't do much for me that day. I had other things on my mind.

You know how something can get stuck in your brain, so that you can't think of anything else? Round and around go your thoughts, with no beginning and no end, leaving you feeling the same way at the end as you felt when you started — or worse.

That's how it was with me that Shabbos afternoon.

I was up in my room pretending to read a book, while all those thoughts were clogging up my brain. Finally, in disgust, I went to the window to stare out at the snow. Not that I really saw it, mind you. The swirling white was only a backdrop for my ongoing — and not very pleasant — thoughts ....

Suddenly, as a welcome break in the middle of all that white, I saw something.

No — I saw some*one.* The someone was walking up the block toward the big corner intersection in front of my house.

It was a girl, I could see that, though it was impossible to tell her age from up here. With her collar turned up and a hat protecting her head from the falling snow, I couldn't get much more than a glimpse of her face. There was snow on her shoulders and on her hat. Where was she going in the middle of a snowstorm?

The girl seemed to be wondering the same thing.

I saw her walk halfway up one block, then turn around and come back to our corner. A few steps up the other block — and back again. Was she a person who simply couldn't make up her mind where she wanted to go? Or was she lost?

I watched some more. Dry and warm in my room, I felt strangely detached from what I was seeing — as though the girl was part of a show, and not a real, live person at all. I saw her stand very still in the middle of the intersection (there were no cars going by in this weather) and gaze in all four directions.

There was something about the way she stood that made me realize, all at once, that she *was* real.

And she obviously was lost.

It took me a few seconds to get my window open. I strained hard until, with a yank, it flew upward. A blast of frigid air slapped me in the face — bringing a couple of handfuls of cold, wet white along with it.

"Good Shabbos!" I called, leaning out.

The girl looked in every direction but the right one. I tried again. "HELLO! UP HERE!"

Finally, she looked up. Seeing me, she broke into a relieved grin.

"Do you need help?" I yelled. The falling snow seemed to muffle sound.

She nodded vigorously. "I'm not sure how to get to my cousin's house!" she shouted. She named a street that was about a ten-minute walk from where she stood.

"That's pretty far to walk in this weather!" I called. Hesitating only a second, I added, "Want to come in and dry out a little, while I tell you how to get there?"

Another vigorous nod, accompanied by a second relieved grin, and she was stomping through the snow to my front door.

By running downstairs, I was on hand to open it even before she got there.

"Thank you!" the girl gasped, as a blast of warm air met her inside the door. She pulled off her hat and shook the snow gingerly onto the mat. Then she stamped her feet to do the same to her boots. "I really appreciate this."

"No problem. Come on up, I'll get you a towel."

With a grateful smile, she followed me up the stairs. I fetched a towel, and then led her to my room so she could drape the towel over herself and slowly dry off. I hung her coat on the shower head in the bathroom so it would drip into the tub, and then returned to my room. The girl had begun to defrost and was looking a lot happier.

"Hi!" she said a little shyly, handing back the towel. "I'm Miri Spielman. I'm staying at my cousin's house because her brother — who's also my cousin — is having a bar mitzvah this Shabbos."

I glanced out the window and shivered. "Some week for a bar mitzvah."

"I know. Anyway, my younger sister wanted to visit a friend she knows from camp, and I volunteered to take her over there. I love walking in the snow …."

"Me, too," I agreed. Though the experience is a lot better when you know where you're going …

"Anyway," she said, getting comfortable on my desk chair, while I perched on my bed, "I got her there okay. It was on my way back that the problems started. I just seemed to be going in circles." Miri sighed. "I have the world's worst sense of direction."

"I saw you out there," I said sympathetically. "Anyone could have gotten confused. All the streets look alike in the snow."

"*And* I'm not from here," she added, "which makes it even more confusing. I have no idea which street leads where."

"Where are you from?"

"Cincinnati. A little smaller than New York …"

I grinned. "A little. So, who's your cousin? Maybe I know her."

"Her name's Yehudis Limber. Know her?"

The dance of the snow outside my window was mesmerizing. Gazing at it, I murmured, "Actually, I do. And I knew that her brother had a bar mitzvah coming up … though I forgot exactly when it was happening."

"Well, it's this Shabbos — just in time for a major snowstorm! We were supposed to start the drive home tonight, but I don't think we'll be going anywhere for a while."

"Well, that's not so bad," I suggested. "You can have fun with your cousin Yehudis till it's time to go."

"Right." There was something about the way she pronounced that syllable — and the turned-down mouth that went with it — that alerted me to the fact that the idea did not exactly thrill her.

"What's the matter?" I asked.

"Oh, Yehudis isn't much fun this weekend. We're more or less the same age, and I was really looking forward to spending some time with my cousin, you know? But she's in such a 'down' mood. She hardly wants to do anything."

This was interesting. "A down mood? Why?"

Before she could answer, there was a commotion at my door and my little brother, Yanky, burst in. "Estie said she saw a snowman walk in before." He looked eagerly around the room. "Where is it?"

Miri laughed. "I guess I'm the snowman your sister saw. I *was* pretty much covered with snow when I walked in."

Yanky looked disappointed. "But you're just a girrul!"

"I guess I am. Sorry ..."

"Yanky, this is Miri," I introduced with a wink at my guest. "Miri, Yanky is very talented at finding *nosh*. Do you want him to go down to the kitchen and find us some?"

"That would be very nice," Miri smiled.

"Yanky, do you think you could find us a big bag of chips by the time I count to fifteen?"

He looked doubtful. "Could you make it twenty-five?"

"You got a deal."

Yanky whirled around and zoomed out the door. Miri and I laughed. I started counting, slowly, to twenty-five. Yanky was back, with a red face and the bag of chips, by twenty-three.

"Good job!" we praised him. Yanky got a handful of chips for his pains, and went away happy.

"Now!" I said, as we munched. "Where were we?"

"I really should be going," Miri said, not budging. "My parents might start to worry." She took another chip.

"You were telling me why your cousin Yehudis is in a bad mood this Shabbos."

"Oh, that. Actually, I think she's been in a bad mood for a while now. You see, she had a fight with her best friend — and they're not talking."

"Oh? How long has this been going on?"

"A couple of weeks, I think. And let me tell you, she's *really* down in the dumps about it. Seems she said something that hurt her friend's feelings, and now she and her friend — her name's Chaya Sara — aren't speaking."

"Is it possible that Yehudis didn't try hard enough to make amends?"

"Oh, she tried," Miri said. "Yehudis told me that she apologized to her friend right away! But Chaya Sara was so hurt that she couldn't hear her."

"Wow, that's … that's really sad."

"Yes, it is. Last night, when we were in bed, she told me about it. And let me tell you, Yehudis is really feeling bad. She wishes she'd never said what she did! But it seems like it's too late now." Miri reached for a last chip and got reluctantly to her feet. "Well, I really appreciate this. But I guess I should get going …"

I stood, too. "I'll tell you how to get to Yehudis' house."

"Thanks. I wish I had a better sense of direction. I get lost *everywhere*! Once, I got lost around the corner from my own house! How embarrassing is that? Of course," she added in her own defense, "I was a lot younger then."

"That's tough," I said sympathetically. "You know, having a good sense of direction is really about … noticing things. If you pay attention to landmarks and things on your way somewhere, then you'll notice them again on your way back. That way, you won't get lost."

Miri sighed. "It sounds so easy when you say it. I guess I'm not such a 'noticing' kind of person."

"Do you really think so? Let's do an experiment!" I said. "An exercise in noticing … Take a quick look at my dresser. Then close your eyes and list five things you saw there."

Looking doubtful, she glanced at my dresser and obediently shut her eyes. "I saw … *umm* … a brush. And … and …" Her eyes flew open. "It's no use. I told you, I'm awful at noticing!"

"Try again," I urged. "This time, take ten seconds to study the dresser. One, two, three — go!"

Miri stared fixedly at the dresser top for the allotted

ten seconds. Then, at my command, she closed her eyes again.

"Now," I said. "What's on my dresser?"

"A brush," she said promptly, "and a headband, and a birthday card, and … a china doll, and … and …"

I held my breath.

"A basket of scrunchies!" she finished, and opened her eyes.

"Excellent!" I exclaimed. "You see? You remembered much more this time. Because you *noticed*."

"Because you told me to. When I'm on my own, I'm usually thinking of something else …."

"Well, remind yourself to notice, and your problems will be over."

Miri smiled at me. "Thanks! I think that's going to be a big help. Now, could you tell me how to get back to my cousin's?"

We stood at the window. "You go up that block and continue straight on till the third streetlight. You'll see a big supermarket on one side and a toy store on the other. Turn right at the toy store, walk two more blocks — and you'll be on Yehudis' corner."

"Thanks! I think I can find it from there." She turned away from the window, and I went to get her coat from the bathroom. It was still damp, but at least the snow had melted.

"Good luck," I said, as she started slipping her arms into the sleeves. I hesitated. "Uh, one more thing …"

"What?" She stopped what she was doing and looked at me.

"Here's some advice for Yehudis. Tell her … tell her to try apologizing again. It's not just the apology that counts, but also when you offer it."

"Which is … when?"

"Well … probably *not* when the person whose feelings you just hurt is still all worked up about it. Maybe later on, when she's had some time to calm down, and to realize how much your friendship means to her — that would be a good time to try again. Because then, she might actually be able to hear you …"

There was admiration in the look Miri gave me. "That sounds like good advice. Just like the tip about noticing landmarks. You sound as if you know what you're talking about."

"That's me," I said lightly, "the wise woman of the block."

She grinned. "Okay, O Wise One. I'll pass it on."

I walked Miri downstairs. "Well, have a safe walk back. Maybe we'll see each other again some time."

"I hope so." At the door, she turned. "You know something? I just realized — I don't even know your name!"

"That *is* funny. How could I have forgotten to tell you? My name is Chaya Sara ...." I smiled. "Have a good Shabbos, Miri ...."

Laizer Takes the Lead

By the time he was twelve years old, Laizer was right where he wanted to be: at the top.

Laizer was a leader. All of his friends followed him obediently as if they were a flock of sheep and he was their shepherd …. Well, maybe not *that* obediently. But there's no question that Laizer was king of his class.

Just why that was so is hard to say. Laizer wasn't the best student in their class; Menachem Finer had that distinction. He also wasn't the best athlete; that was definitely Dovid Brenner. What Laizer had was the kind of personality that naturally attracted others to fall in line behind him. He had ideas, and he had the energy to make them happen. A leader.

Yes, Laizer was on top of the world … until the day his father broke the news that turned Laizer's world upside-down.

•◎•◎•

"My company is transferring me to a small city in the Midwest," he told his family that night. "The new job comes with a big raise in pay, which our family can certainly use. But I'm afraid it will mean moving away from your schools and your friends."

Laizer's sisters took it pretty well, all things considered. After an initial few days of weeping and wailing, they settled down to plan their new life in the new place. They started to pelt their parents with questions about the house and the school. They didn't seem too worried about fitting in. There were four of them, and they would be companions for each other during the transition period before they made new friends.

Laizer wasn't so lucky. All he had was a baby brother who wasn't anywhere near ready for school yet. Even worse, he would have to give up his cherished position at the top of the ladder. He would have to start all over again in a new place.

"Don't worry," his mother comforted him as they packed up the house in preparation for the big move. "You're the kind of boy who makes friends easily. I'm sure you'll feel comfortable in no time."

His father consoled him in a more practical way: by buying Laizer a brand-new, ten-speed bike. "Our new home is in a suburban area. That means parks and woods and lots of space for riding bikes." Laizer had to admit he was looking forward to that.

Moving day was a brilliant Monday morning in early July. Laizer and his sisters would be going to camp in August. This first month was for getting to know their new town.

The ride was long and monotonous. Halfway through it, Laizer fell asleep. When he awoke, he found that the car had pulled up in front of a pleasant-looking white house with a big lawn and the rosy glint of flowers. It didn't look too bad.

A few minutes' investigation showed him that the inside was fine, too. He liked his room, and there was a good home for his new bike inside the garage. That night passed in an exhausted blur. The next day was spent unpacking and positioning furniture — and then repositioning it when Ma decided she'd made a mistake the first time. By the time the sun had set on their first full day in their new home, Laizer was feeling cautiously optimistic. So far, so good.

Then he met some of the neighborhood kids, and the problems began.

The problem was that the boys already had a leader. His name was Shmulie.

Shmulie Holtzer was an outgoing, outspoken kid with red hair and an engaging personality. When he suggested a course of action, the other kids were eager to carry it out. The first few times Laizer broached an idea, it was as if he hadn't spoken. The others were too used to following *their* leader to pay much attention to another, would-be leader. Especially when he was the new boy in town.

Laizer didn't like the situation. But what, he wondered as he pedaled his bike slowly around the block, could he do about it?

A few of the neighborhood fathers had arranged for their boys to learn with a tutor in the mornings, and Laizer's father quickly signed him up, too. It was a good way to meet kids his age. The afternoons were reserved for swimming, biking, playing ball or whatever else might take the fancy of a vigorous group of twelve-year-old boys.

At dinner that night, Laizer's father remarked, "I hear there's a nice park with hiking trails not too far from here, Laizer. Why don't you and your friends bike over there tomorrow?"

"You could make a picnic," Ma added.

It sounded good to Laizer. But *he* wasn't the one who decided such things anymore. He prowled around the house, and then went out to kick a soccer ball in the backyard. This feeling of helplessness — of being a follower instead of a leader — did not sit well with him. He climbed a tree and scowled down at the world.

Maybe it was the different point of view provided by his perch in the tree that made Laizer decide to approach the problem from a different angle. He wanted to go biking with the other kids in Pine Ridge Park. The only way that was likely to happen was if it got

Shmulie's stamp of approval. Should he call Shmulie?

Laizer thought this over, and then he shook his head. He had a better idea.

A minute later, he'd scrambled down the trunk and shot back into the house. He looked up Yitzy Shulman's number. Yitzy was a nice kid in their learning group.

"Hey, Yitzy. It's Laizer."

"Hey, Laizer." Yitzy sounded surprised to hear from him. "What's up?"

"I hear there's a fantastic park not far away — Pine Ridge. Ever hear of it?"

"Hear of it! I've been there millions of times."

Correctly assessing this as an exaggeration, Laizer plowed on. "Want to go tomorrow? We could take along some sandwiches and have a picnic."

"Uh … I'm not sure. It sounds like a good idea, but …"

But you can't decide a thing like that without Shmulie's okay, Laizer thought cynically. "Okay, forget it," he said. "It was just a thought. See ya tomorrow …"

As Laizer had hoped, his "thought" quickly took root in Yitzy's mind. It led Yitzy to make a phone call of his own — to Shmulie Holtzer. One thing led to another, until Shmulie announced that he had a great idea for an outing tomorrow: a bike ride to Pine Ridge Park!

"We'll have a picnic," he decided. "Start a chain call, Yitz. We leave right after learning."

Laizer, at the end of the chain, smiled at the news. It was a rather grim smile. He didn't like being at the tail end of anything — let alone an idea that had been *his* in the first place! But "Count me in!" was all he said. Then he went along to the kitchen to fix some sandwiches and snacks for the trip.

The weather cooperated perfectly. The next morning dawned fair and clear, with just a hint of a perky breeze to make the long bike ride more fun.

Early in the ride, Laizer took the lead. He was a good biker and had lots of stamina. He'd had his fill of trailing along behind the others. He was going to try to get back to the place where he belonged — at the head instead of the tail. Shmulie or no Shmulie!

Several times, Shmulie tried to overtake him, but Laizer held onto his lead. As they entered the large, sprawling park, he heard Shmulie tell the others that he wanted to ride along the park trails for a while before breaking for lunch.

"I'm getting kinda tired," Mendy Feinberg protested. "Can't we eat now?"

"As soon as we find a good place," Shmulie said.

They biked on, past a small lake and a big playground. The trees were lush and shady, fanning Laizer's face as he pedaled for all he was worth. Suddenly, the paths diverged. To his right, Laizer glimpsed a cool glade and heard the sound of running water. A creek! Here was a fine place to have their lunch.

"There's water over there, guys!" he called out. "C'mon!" He steered his bike to the right.

But Shmulie, coming up to the fork in the path next, steered left. And the others, naturally, followed right along behind him …

Before he knew it, Laizer found himself riding alone through the trees.

The silence sounded like thunder in his ears. No one had followed him. Instead, they had all gone where Shmulie had led. Laizer was mortified. He was mad. Most of all, he was bewildered.

He felt like a king whose throne had been stolen right out from under him.

Until this moment, deep down he'd believed it was only a matter of time before he'd take his natural place at the head of the pack. All of this was just a temporary setback. Any day now, the other kids would recognize him as their leader, just like the kids back home ….

But nobody had followed him. It seemed like a symbol of everything that was wrong with his life since the move. Laizer had lost his secure place at the top. He had gone right, and they'd gone left.

He reached the creek, but didn't stop. He wanted to keep moving forever. He never wanted to face the other kids again. He rode parallel to the creek for a while, and then veered off onto another trail. On impulse, he jumped off his bike and kicked an innocent tree that just happened to be in the wrong place at the wrong time.

"Watch out. You can break your toes that way," a voice said mildly from behind.

Laizer spun around. He was in a clearing, with a circle of park benches surrounding a pretty little fountain in the center. Birds hopped on the rim and drank from the pooled water in the fountain. On one of the benches sat the elderly man who had just spoken to him. Laizer remembered seeing him in shul. He didn't know the man's name, and he sure didn't want to talk to him — or anyone — right now. This was *definitely* not his day .... "Sorry," he muttered.

"No need to apologize to *me*," the old man smiled. "It's *your* toes I'm thinking about." He peered at the boy. "You look upset. Anything I can do to help?"

Laizer shook his head. He longed to get back on his bike and sail away, but he didn't want to be rude.

The old man patted the bench beside him. "Have

a seat. Get a load off your feet," he invited. "*And* your mind …"

Reluctantly, Laizer sat. "It's nothing," he muttered, staring at the ground.

"You seem pretty down in the dumps over 'nothing.'"

Laizer hesitated. Under the man's grandfatherly gaze, he suddenly found himself eager to unburden himself. The words were weighing on his heart, and spilling them out would feel good. Why not tell him?

"Well … it's like this. I'm new here. We just moved to this town. Back home, I had tons of friends … and I was sort of the leader, know what I mean? But here …" Laizer's voice trailed off.

"Here, you're just one of the crowd," the man said. "At least, I hope you are." He peered at Laizer from under grizzled brows. "You *have* made friends, haven't you?"

"Yes. Some kids from the neighborhood."

"Good. So you feel uncomfortable being in the middle of the pack, instead of at the head of it."

Laizer flushed again. "Something like that." Before he knew it, he was pouring out the whole story. It ended with him urging the others to follow him rightward, to the creek — and the others steering their bikes leftward, in Shmulie's wake.

The old man was silent for a few moments,

considering the problem. "Want to hear what I think?" he asked presently. Without waiting for Laizer to answer, he went on. "A leader is not simply born that way. He has to work for his position. It's about more than just grabbing power, you know."

"I don't want *power*, exactly," Laizer said. "I just want the other kids to listen to my ideas."

"It's about wisdom," the man continued, as if Laizer hadn't spoken. "It's about dignity."

Wisdom? Dignity? Those were serious words. Laizer frowned, trying to bend his brain around them.

"It's about being compassionate toward those who follow you," the man said reflectively. He sent a piercing glance at Laizer. "Most of all, it's about becoming the kind of person that people *want* to follow."

A few minutes of uncomfortable silence followed this speech. Laizer cleared his throat. "Um — thanks."

"You *will* thank me, one day," the man predicted. "When you've figured out what it is I'm trying to tell you."

"I guess so …."

"And one other thing …," the man added, as if as an afterthought.

Laizer glanced at him questioningly.

"Is it really so bad being in the middle of the pack once in a while?"

Laizer didn't answer. He wasn't sure what to say.

The old man leaned back in his seat, suddenly tired. "Go ahead — find your friends," he said with a smile. "And remember what we talked about. I think you'll find it helpful."

"Well, thanks again ...." Bidding the man a polite farewell, Laizer climbed back on his bike and began retracing his route back along the trail.

He heard them before he saw them.

Off to the left, in a sunny clearing, picnic tables were arranged along an arm of the lake they'd passed earlier. The boys were busy demolishing their sandwiches.

"Hi, Laizer!" Yitzy Shulman called out. One or two of the other boys waved a greeting as well. Laizer waved back, washed his hands and joined them.

"Where'd you disappear to?" Shmulie asked around a bite of tuna fish sandwich.

Dignity, the old man had recommended. So instead of being sulky or flippant or otherwise broadcasting his displeasure at the way things had turned out, Laizer merely said, "I went exploring. Nice creek."

Shmulie nodded. "It *is* nice. But Mendy was *sta-a-arving*." He glanced sideways at Mendy with a grin.

The picnic over, the boys bentched and got back on

their bikes. They practiced skimming stones on the lake and explored several more trails, and then it was time to go. As they pointed their bikes homeward, Laizer asked, "By the way — where's Chaim today?"

"He had a virus this weekend," Mendy told him. "He wanted to come biking with us today, but his mother thought it would be too much for him."

It's about being compassionate, the old man had suggested.

Slowly, Laizer said, "I guess I'll go over to Chaim's house when we get back. He must be pretty lonely."

One or two of the other boys looked surprised. Yitzy said, "You know, I think I'll join you." And Dovy Mandelbaum said, "Me, too."

It's about becoming the kind of person that people want to follow.

Yitzy and Dovy flanked Laizer on the ride home, chatting with him and getting to know him better. Ahead of them, Shmulie was in the lead. Laizer was not where he wanted to be, at the head of the pack, but that was okay. The middle felt pretty good, too.

It had been a strange, mixed-up sort of day. Maybe, in time, things would be the way they used to be. Maybe Laizer would wear the crown again … but only if he went about it the right way. Not by seizing power — but by earning it.

A few of the boys broke away as they reached Chaim's corner, calling good-bye over their shoulders. Yitzy, Dovy and Laizer continued straight on.

"Last one there's a rotten egg!" Laizer shouted, and began pedaling for all he was worth. Behind him, the other boys struggled to keep up. Laizer got there first. He dismounted, propped up his bike and waited for the others.

Then he led the way to Chaim's front door, and his new friends followed right behind.

Molly's Mystery Day

"Malya Tova Binderman! What do you think you're doing?"

Molly flinched as her big sister's angry face appeared in her doorway. Nobody called her by her full name unless she was in major trouble.

"Uh … nothing?" she tried.

"*Nothing*? Do you call it 'nothing' when you blast your music so loud that it wakes the baby — after I just spent *forty-five* minutes getting her to sleep?"

"Oops." Molly looked abashed. She reached out and turned off the CD player on her desk.

"You can say that again. Plus a *big* apology."

"Sorry, Ahuva. I didn't realize the music was on so loud."

"That's the whole trouble — you never realize anything! You are so oblivious, Molly."

"Oblivious to what?" Molly asked in puzzlement.

"Oblivious to *everything*!"

With that, Ahuva walked out of Molly's room — stopping herself just in time from slamming the door and startling the baby as she was trying to fall asleep again ….

Left alone, Molly replayed the scene in her head for a moment. Ahuva always got so steamed up over things. With a shrug, she pushed the whole thing out of her mind. She put away her school books — she'd finished her homework while listening to the CD — picked up her newest library book, and settled down to an enjoyable half hour of reading before bed.

•◎•◎•

Unfortunately, the half hour turned into two hours. Molly was consequently testy and overtired as she trudged off to school the next morning.

As usual, she waited for her friend Gitty to meet her on the corner so they could walk to school together. And, as usual, Gitty was late.

As Gitty came up the street toward Molly, this is what she saw: critical eyes and a downturned mouth. A face, as the saying goes, that could sour milk … She ventured a tentative "Hi," but all she got for her trouble was a snapped "You're late!"

"I know," Gitty said contritely. "Sorry about that. My mother made me eat breakfast."

"My mother makes *me* eat breakfast every morning. And *I'm* not late!"

"I *said* I was sorry."

Molly remembered an expression she'd once heard her uncle use. "That and a dime'll buy me a cup of coffee …."

Gitty was startled. "Huh? Who said anything about

coffee? I had cornflakes for breakfast."

Molly rolled her eyes and started walking, fast. Gitty had to hurry to keep up with her. By this time, she was smarting from her friend's snappish manner and her own temper was becoming a bit frayed. By the time they arrived at school, neither girl was speaking to the other.

The day got no better as it went on. Right in the middle of *Chumash* class, Molly dropped her looseleaf onto the floor and watched in dismay as its contents scattered far and wide. As a few of her classmates began helpfully collecting papers with her, Morah Feingold made a disapproving face. "Malya, this is the third time that's happened. Can't you keep your looseleaf on your desk in such a way that it doesn't keep falling and disturbing our class?"

"Sorry," Molly mumbled.

"It's not enough to be sorry. You have to solve the problem!"

"I'll try, Morah."

When the looseleaf had been reassembled and quiet restored to the classroom, Molly sat back in her seat and tried to pay attention. This was not easy, as she was feeling very sorry for herself at the moment. What a miserable day this was turning out to be! Starting with her fight with Gitty this morning …

No, even before that. Starting with her big sister

yelling at her last night. With a sense of "poor me," Molly ripped a page out of her looseleaf and began writing a note to Gitty, who sat one row over from her own seat.

Gitty averted her head and would not accept the note. Angrily, Molly passed it instead to another friend who was seated just in front of her.

"I'll take that, Malya." It was Morah Feingold, and she was not happy. The teacher stretched out her hand to take the note.

With a sigh, Molly handed it over. The "poor me" feeling was even stronger than before.

•◎•◎•

This would be her second detention this month! Molly fumed as she walked home later that day. She would have to spend her lunch period tomorrow in a room all by herself. *Poor me!*

Once she was back home, she found her spirits rising. The school day was behind her and she could relax. She started by picking up the next book in the series she'd started the night before. She was comfortably curled up on the couch with it when her mother reminded her that it was her turn to set the table.

"Can't someone else do it?" Molly whined. "Ahuva or Bentzi? I'm kind of busy …."

"You can read later," Ma said calmly. "Set the table, Molly. Supper's almost ready."

After supper, while her brother cleared the table and her sister washed the dishes, Molly played with the baby until the phone rang. It was Gitty.

Molly's heart lifted. She hurried to the phone and exclaimed, "Gitty! What's doing?"

"Oh, nothing much," Gitty said casually. *In other words, "You're forgiven."*

Molly had forgiven her, too. It was too hard getting through the day without her best friend to talk things over with. She proceeded to regale Gitty with the details of her miserable day. "And to top it all off," she moaned, "we had an awful supper. Meatloaf!" She made a gagging sound.

"We had barbecued chicken," Gitty said.

"Yum! I *love* your mother's barbecued chicken. It's the best!"

A voice at her elbow made Molly turn in surprise. "If you're nearly done, Molly, I need to make a call."

The voice was cool. Ma was clearly displeased about something.

It occurred to Molly — a few seconds too late — that her mother must have overheard her less-than-complimentary comments about her cooking just now. Molly had certainly made no effort to lower her voice … Hastily, she said good-bye to Gitty.

After she'd hung up the phone, Molly considered apologizing to her mother. But Ma was busy making her phone call — and anyway, the whole thing was way too awkward. Molly pushed the whole thing out of her mind and went back to her room with her homework and her new book.

She'd finished her homework and was just getting comfortable with her book when her brother Bentzi barged into her room. "Molly, I need my CD back."

"Have you ever heard of knocking?"

"Right, but there's no time. My friend Shmulie's on his way over to borrow my new CD. I lent it to you to listen to yesterday, remember? Now I need it back."

"Oh, right." Molly got up and went to the CD player. Bentzi's CD was not insidc. She frowned. "I listened to it right after school. Then I put in something else …."

"Well, where's mine?" he asked impatiently.

That was a good question. Molly began searching the area around her CD player. Then she scanned the floor beneath her desk and farther afield. By the time she found the dusty CD under her bed, Shmulie had arrived and both he and Bentzi were annoyed at the delay.

The moment his friend left, Bentzi gave his sister a piece of his mind. Bentzi was quite articulate and his tongue could be sharp. The instant he was gone, Molly promptly burst into tears. What a *really* awful day this was turning out to be. *Poor, poor me!*

Ahuva was up to her eyeballs in algebra equations, but she took the time out to knock on her sister's door a little later that evening. She felt badly about the way she'd yelled at Molly the night before, and wanted to apologize.

She found Molly huddled under her covers, sobbing.

"Molly! What's the matter? What's wrong?" Ahuva sat down on the edge of her sister's bed.

An incoherent sentence floated up out of the covers.

"I can't understand you, Molly. Come on … sit up and talk to me."

Eventually, Molly was able to speak. "I had a t-terrible day. It actually started with you yelling at me last night."

"I'm sorry about that. That's why I came in just now."

"Well, okay … But then, this morning, I had a fight with Gitty on the way to school. And my teacher yelled at me in *Chumash* class, and Ma got upset because I criticized her cooking, and Bentzi yelled at me for losing his CD — even though I found it again. It's been such a h-horrible day … and I don't even know why! Everything seems to go wrong somehow. It's a real mystery!"

Ahuva thought she knew why, but she wasn't sure if Molly was capable of really hearing it. "Maybe it's not such a mystery, Molly. Maybe there are good reasons why these things happen to you."

"I never mean to do anything wrong! But people are always getting mad at me …"

"Well, you *are* a little — self-centered, shall we call it?"

Molly looked up, her eyes damp and her cheeks tear-stained. "What?"

"Remember when I called you 'oblivious'? You tend to go your merry way, without realizing how your actions impact on the people around you. But they *do* impact people … and then the people get mad. Get it?"

It was obvious that Molly didn't get it. She gazed at her big sister with a woebegone expression. With a sigh, Ahuva said, "Well, here's some advice. Whatever you're thinking about doing — do the opposite. That should do the trick."

Molly stared. "Are you serious?"

"Yup. Try it for a day. Tomorrow, do the opposite of whatever it is you would have done. And see what happens!" Ahuva glanced at the desk clock. "I'd better get back to my room and finish studying for my big math test tomorrow."

"Good luck."

Ahuva made a face. "I'm sure going to need it …." She left.

Molly was too tired to think about what Ahuva had just said. She was too tired to think about anything. She was even too tired to read. She quickly got ready for bed, thankful to drop a curtain of sleep over the whole miserable day.

When she woke the next morning, Molly remembered her sister's advice. With the memory of yesterday's string of fiascos behind her, she decided she had nothing to lose. *I'll try it!* she thought.

She was about to rattle off "*Modeh Ani*" without thinking, the way she did every morning, when she stopped. It was time to do — the opposite. So she slowed down and recited the words with real meaning. Feeling happy and peaceful at this good start, she jumped out of bed to start her day.

Breakfast that morning was French toast. Molly remembered her friend Gitty's comment about cornflakes. Ma really spent a lot of time and energy preparing

delicious breakfasts for her kids. Molly would normally have shoveled down the French toast without comment — but this was "opposite day." So she smiled at her mother and said, "This is absolutely the best French toast in the world, Ma. Delicious!"

Her mother's tired face lit up as if someone had switched on a bulb inside. "Thank you, Molly! That's kind of you to say."

"It's kind of *you* to go to all this trouble for us. Thanks!" With a quick kiss, Molly was out the door and on her way to school.

But first, there was Gitty to meet at the corner. Once again, the corner was empty when Molly got there. Molly started rehearsing lines in her head. This was the second day in a row that her friend was late. She would really lash into her now!

Then she remembered — do the opposite. So when Gitty came running breathlessly up a few minutes later, Molly was all smiles. "No problem, Gitty. Let's hurry, though, or we'll be late!"

Gitty was so thankful to have been spared a tongue-lashing that she agreed to play "Twenty Questions" with Molly all the way to school — one of Molly's favorite games.

In *Chumash* class, Molly was about to lay her loose-leaf any-which-way on her desk, when she recalled yesterday's disaster. Carefully, she positioned it more securely. And she did *not* send off a single note, to Gitty or anyone else, but sat quietly attentive. Opposite day!

The results were opposite of the day's before, too. Morah Feingold actually smiled at her, and then she picked her to go down to the office with a message for the secretary.

That afternoon, when she got home, Molly made a beeline for the fridge to get something to snack on before supper. She found her brother right next to her, intent on the same thing. Bentzi shouldered her aside and rummaged through the food on the shelves.

"Excuse me!" Molly said indignantly. She was about to add "I was here first!" and create a scene, when she remembered her sister's advice. And so, swallowing the words, she said again, in a very different voice, "Excuse me"— and stepped aside to give her brother more room.

To her surprise, Bentzi emerged from the fridge with not one, but two, fruit yogurts. He handed her one. "Here. It's your favorite flavor."

Molly beamed. "Thanks a lot!"

The yogurt was good. But the glow in her heart was much, much better …

That night, while doing her homework, Molly was in the mood for music. She put a CD into her player and was about to press the "Play" button — when she remembered the baby who was probably just dropping off to sleep. She lowered the volume dramatically before starting the music.

All this reminded her of Ahuva. Usually, her thoughts of Ahuva centered around herself — what she wanted to ask Ahuva to do for her and the like. Tonight, in the grip of "opposite day," Molly suddenly remembered the big math test her big sister had been so nervous about the night before. She must have taken the test today. Molly decided to pay a visit to Ahuva's room to find out how it had gone.

The visit went well. In fact, it went so well that Molly went to bed that night feeling something extraordinary.

For the first time in her life, she felt her own power to make other people feel happier.

She'd made Ma happy, and her teacher pleased. She'd made the kind of choices that put her on a more harmonious footing with her brother and her sister. She'd even helped the baby fall asleep! And all because she'd stopped for a second to think before doing the usual thing.

All because, for the space of a single day, she'd stopped being oblivious.

It was a heady feeling. It was so good that Molly

thought she just might try a repeat of "opposite day" tomorrow. Starting right now …

Remembering how grumpy she'd been on too little sleep, she resolutely put aside her exciting new book when the clock told her it was time. It wasn't easy, but it felt right.

As she drifted into a contented sleep, Molly sent a silent "thank You" up to the One Who gives every single person in the world the power to choose one thing … or its opposite!

Cover for Me

Don't get me wrong — I'm as independent as the next kid. I can function perfectly well on my own. It's just that, most of the time, I don't care to. Is it my fault that I enjoy things more when I'm doing them with my friends?

Especially my best friend, Hilly.

Hilly was sitting right beside me as the bus pulled away from the curb and started the long trip up to camp. I twisted in my seat for a last wave at my mother and father, swallowed a sudden lump in my throat and turned back to my friend. "Well, this is it."

"Yeah. I can't wait!" Hilly had never been to camp before. It was my second season.

"I'll show you the ropes," I offered. "By the time I'm through with you, no one will ever guess this is your first time in camp."

I must admit, Hilly didn't need much coaching. He took to camp the way a fish takes to water. There were nine boys in our bunk; by the end of the first day, he knew everyone's name by heart. By the end of the first night, he was friends with them all. It took me a little longer. Unlike Hilly, I'm a bit shy around strangers and it takes me some time to warm up to them. It must have been all of three or four days into camp before I'd sorted out all my bunkmates and knew who was who.

Five of them were just like Hilly and me: thrilled to be there and eager to have a great time. The other two stood out like sore thumbs. Or rather, sore campers. Their names were Yossi and Baruch.

Yossi's father was a high-powered businessman whose business enterprises took him all over the world. This summer, he and Yossi's mother were off on a three-continent tour that would last five or six weeks. They had arranged to send all of their children to camp during that time. Their four daughters went happily enough. But not Yossi.

"This is the last place I want to be," he muttered on our first night in camp, as we lay listening to the crickets creak and the mosquitoes whine. "I wanted to go with my parents, but they said there'd be nothing for me to do over there. So I begged them to let me go to my cousin in Denver for the summer. But would they let me? No way." He shook his head in the dark. "Does anyone care about what *I* want? Nope. Off they shipped me to camp ..."

"I'm with you," Baruch declared. "I hate camp. I hate sports and I hate swimming and I hate camp food."

"Where would you rather be instead?" I asked drowsily.

"Anywhere!"

With that kind of attitude, it's no wonder that both

Yossi and Baruch soon got on our counselor's nerves. Zalmy tried to be understanding, but it's hard to sympathize when two of your campers are on a campaign to drive you bananas. Or at least, that's the way it felt to Zalmy.

Every day, it seemed, Baruch and Yossi got themselves into another scrape. They played pranks. They either came late to activities or skipped them altogether. They refused to join in the games on the ball field and declined to sing in the dining room. Their favorite activity seemed to be complaining. In short, they were a royal pain in the neck.

For some reason, Hilly liked them.

"I don't mind their kvetching," he told me once. "I feel kind of sorry for them."

"I feel sorrier for *us*," I said. "It's no fun having kids in your bunk who'd rather be anywhere else."

Hilly shrugged. "I don't know about that. They're okay, once you get to know them …."

Personally, I had no desire to get to know them. I was perfectly happy doing what everyone else in camp was doing: having a blast. Though I never admitted it to Hilly, secretly I also felt a little sorry for Yossi and Baruch. It's tough being shipped off to a place you don't like for eight long weeks. But miserable as they were, did they have to be so annoyingly negative all the time?

Apparently, the answer to that was "yes." On they went, making trouble and then patiently enduring the lectures they received in return. Zalmy would give them a scolding and then pass them on to the head counselor for some more. But none of it really seemed to penetrate. Yossi and Baruch went right on, the same way as before.

One night, Hilly came to me in great excitement.

"There's something going on tonight. I need you to cover for me."

"What's going on?"

"Uh, it's sort of a secret …."

I put on my stubborn face. "Either you tell me, or you're on your own."

"Okay, okay. Just don't tell anyone else, all right? The head counselor told Baruch and Yossi that he's reaching the end of his patience. Any more trouble from them, he warned, and they're O-U-T … out!" Hillel mimicked the head counselor's voice perfectly.

"So?" I asked sarcastically. "Isn't that exactly what they want?"

"Oh, he's always saying things like that. But you know those two. They want to have fun their own way. So, tonight …"

I waited. At last, I prompted, "Tonight?"

"Tonight," Hilly whispered, "they're going to have

some *real* fun. They're planning to go down to the lake and race canoes in the dark!"

I drew back. "That's dangerous!"

"Oh, they'll be careful. There's no wind, and they've canoed across the lake a million times already."

"During the day," I pointed out.

"So what? It's the same thing."

I wasn't so sure. "If they get caught, there'll be real trouble."

"Who'll see us?"

"*Us*?" I froze.

Hilly looked sheepish and defiant at the same time. "I'm going with them."

"Why in the world are *you* going?"

"They need a referee …."

I tried to talk him out of it. I told him that what they were contemplating was dangerous. I told him he was courting trouble. But Hilly was not exactly what I'd call receptive to my warnings. In fact, it would not be going too far to say that my words went in one ear and right out the other.

I was about to launch on a second round, when we heard voices. We were about to have company.

"*Shh!*" Hilly whispered urgently. "I'm going to sneak down to the lake right after lights-out. Cover for me!"

There was a lot more I wanted to tell him, but I was

out of time. Our counselor and bunkmates were with us, and it was time to get ready for bed. When lights-out sounded, Zalmy said good night, urged us not to stay up too late, and left the cabin.

Baruch and Yossi slipped out a few minutes later. They took Hilly with them. Hilly threw me a meaningful glance, but I turned my head and looked the other way.

No one will ever know who would have won that after-dark race. Baruch and Yossi, in two separate canoes, had just about reached the midway point in the lake when a stern voice shouted for them to turn around and come back.

It was the head counselor, and he was *mad*. Yossi and Baruch maneuvered their canoes in one-hundred-eighty degree circles until they were facing the direction they'd come from. Then they slowly started paddling ashore.

They found the head counselor waiting for them, a look of fury on his face and one hand gripping Hilly by the arm. All three of them were marched back to the office, where they were treated to a thundering scolding. The next morning, Baruch and Yossi were packing their bags for the trip home. Because it was Hilly's first offense, and he had not actually been out on the lake, he got off with just the scolding.

"I'm glad," Baruch said as he shoved his Shabbos shoes into his duffel bag. "I never wanted to be here in the first place!"

"Me, too." Yossi's parents, off in Europe somewhere, had been tracked down, and had sent instructions for him to take a bus back into the city, where his grandparents would meet him. From there, Yossi hoped, he would be sent off to his cousin in Denver. So it looked like a happy ending for both of them.

It wasn't very happy for Hilly, though. His face was stony as he watched his new friends pack.

"How did the head counselor find out?" he wondered aloud for the tenth time. "It was a dead secret."

The other boys in our bunk were just as mystified as Hilly. All of them, that is, except me. I knew how the head counselor had found out. He'd learned about the race from my counselor Zalmy.

And Zalmy had learned it from me.

To this day, I'm not sure if I would have had the guts to leave the cabin and find the head counselor on my own that night. As it turned out, I didn't have to.

I lay in bed after Hilly and the others left, picturing

the lake, and the two canoes venturing out in the dark, and all the awful things that could happen to the boys riding in them. I clenched my fists as my anxiety mounted. Hilly was to be the referee, he'd told me. Would he and the others go joyriding when the race was over? Would they get rowdy and upset the canoes? Hilly wasn't a very good swimmer ....

I'd just reached this point in my horrified imagining, when the cabin door opened and our counselor walked in. "Forgot something," he said cheerfully, rummaging around on his shelf.

I shot out of bed and darted over to him in the dimness. "Zalmy!" I whispered.

He turned. "What are you doing out of bed after lights-out?"

"I've got something to tell you ...."

It's hard to keep a secret in camp. Zalmy had said he wouldn't tell anyone that I was the one who'd spilled the beans about the race — but, somehow, by the end of the day everyone knew. Hillel stormed up to me with as ugly a look as I'd ever seen him wear.

"Is it true?"

"Is what true?"

"Don't play games with me! Did you tell Zalmy about the race? Is that why Baruch and Yossi were kicked out?"

I hesitated. "I had to, Hilly. What they were doing was dangerous. And you were involved …"

Without another word, he turned and walked away. I stared at my best friend's retreating back with hot, miserable eyes.

How had everything gone so wrong, so fast?

Those were the last words Hilly spoke to me for three long days.

I'd seen him angry before — but never this angry. He wouldn't look at me. He wouldn't answer me when I addressed him. He acted as if I didn't exist.

And, in a way, that's how I felt. Without Hilly, I was only half there.

We'd been best friends since first grade. I was used to us doing just about everything together. As I stomped gloomily down the hill to the pool on the third day, I thought about how happy I'd been with Hilly next to me on the bus ride up to camp. Had it only been two weeks ago? It felt like another lifetime. In that lifetime I'd been on top of the world, with my friend at my side ….

That night, I politely asked Hilly to pass the salt, and he ignored me. I asked again. This time he brushed his cheek, as though a pesky insect had bumbled past it. That made me mad. After supper, when we were instructed to return to our bunks for sweatshirts and flashlights for the night activity, I managed to come up behind Hilly without his noticing. I skirted quickly around him, blocking his way.

"Hey!" he said, going red in the face.

"I just want to talk," I said — or rather, pleaded.

His answer was to shoulder me aside and sprint ahead in the darkness. He moved so fast that he reached the cabin in record time. What Hilly didn't know was that I'd taken a shortcut and gotten there a few seconds before him.

He burst through the door and saw me waiting for him. Both of us were working hard to catch our breaths. With a glare, he spun around to leave. But I grabbed his arm before he could get very far.

"Wait!" I said. "Hilly, why aren't you talking to me?"

He glared some more. "You know why!"

"No, I really don't. What'd I do that was so wrong?"

He shook his head as though he couldn't believe what he was hearing. "And you call yourself a friend!" He tried to wrench free, but I held on tight.

"That depends," I said, "on how you define the word 'friend' … Why are you so mad at me?"

"Do you need me to spell it out? I asked you to cover for me — and you went and told on us!"

I looked him in the eye. "I did cover for you."

"What are you talking about?"

"If I let go, will you hear me out?"

He hesitated. "Just for a second." Despite himself, he was curious.

I let go of Hilly's arm and held out my two hands, palms up. "Let the race go on as planned," I said, lowering one hand as though something as light as a marble had dropped into my palm. "Or stop the race, and prevent my best friend and two other boys from possibly drowning, *chas v'shalom*," I said, lowering my other hand as if a ten-pound weight had dropped on it. "*Hmm* ... Wonder which one a *friend* would do?"

Before Hilly could respond, into the cabin piled the rest of the bunk, plus Zalmy. Hilly rushed away to get his flashlight and didn't talk to me again that night.

Or the next day ...

I'd tried. I'd given it my best shot, and Hilly hadn't understood. He wanted nothing to do with me anymore. I was on my own.

Like I said, I'm okay on my own. I'm as independent as the next kid. But fun, it wasn't ...

When the head counselor announced a surprise trip

to a country fair, I wasn't very excited. He might as well have led us into a barren desert for all I cared. I climbed aboard one of the buses and took a seat by the window — though I can't say I was looking forward to the view. Or the trip. In fact, I wasn't looking forward to much of anything for the rest of the summer.

When someone slid in next to me, I didn't even bother turning my eyes away from the window. Then a familiar voice asked, "This seat taken?"

It was Hilly.

I turned around, astonished and wary. "You?"

Hilly's face was bright pink. He spoke in a rush. "I've been thinking things over, and … and I guess you were right. What we did *was* dangerous. So I guess you had to tell someone about it."

I didn't realize I'd been holding my breath until I let it all out in a long, relieved sigh. "So … we're okay again?"

"That depends," he said, with a sideways look, "on how you define 'okay.'"

This, I thought with a silly grin. Hilly sitting next to me as we set out on a great trip — that was the best definition of "okay" that I could think of.

But all I said was, "I guess you can have the seat — seeing as all the others on the bus are taken."

And he said, "Thanks. And I guess you can have

some of my gum" — he held out a pack — "seeing as I've got plenty to go around."

I took the gum and settled back in my seat. *Absolutely* okay!

Designer Personality

Mrs. Weissman walked through her front door juggling various shopping bags. She'd spent hours in the stores, taking advantage of the end-of-season sales to buy clothing for her children.

There were pants for the boys, and shirts and socks. They would take one look at the new things — if that much — and toss them into their dresser drawers. No, her sons would pose no problem for Mrs. Weissman today.

That job belonged to her only daughter, Tzirel.

As though on cue, Tzirel herself came traipsing down the stairs. "Hi, Ma," she called. She eyed the shopping bags. "Find anything interesting?"

"I certainly did," Mrs. Weissman replied. "I got clothes for the boys — and for you."

Tzirel's eyes lit up. Then the light faded, to be replaced by a look of caution. "Really? Can I see them?"

"Sure. Just give me a minute …."

It was considerably longer than a minute before Tzirel's mother had a chance to show her what she'd bought. Her arrival home brought her children out in force — all five of Tzirel's younger brothers, from ten-year-old Shloimy to three-year-old Chezky. There were hungry mouths to feed and stories to listen to and arguments to arbitrate. By the time the smoke cleared,

Tzirel was nowhere to be seen. Mrs. Weissman assumed that she was back in her room. She was about to start upstairs when Tzirel came clattering down.

"Can I see them now, Ma?" she asked eagerly.

Her mother smiled. "Thanks for your patience, Tzirel." She reached into a pink shopping bag. "I bought this on sale in a good store. It looks like just your style ..." Pulling out a matching skirt and top in a color that was very "today," she held them up.

Tzirel took the skirt and top from her mother and studied them with compressed lips. Clearly, this was *not* the outfit of her dreams.

"What's the matter?" Ma asked.

"I wanted a designer outfit," Tzirel said. "All the girls in my class are wearing designer clothes this year."

"Since when does a sixth-grader need designer clothes?" demanded her brother Shloimy. Tzirel hadn't noticed him lounging on the couch with a book.

"Since now," she said loftily. She turned back to her mother. "Ma, *everyone* wears clothes with a designer logo — or at least a designer label. Why can't I?"

"First of all," her mother said, "I don't believe that 'everyone' is wearing them."

"Well, the popular girls are. And they're the ones that count!"

"Girls are pathetic," Shloimy announced to no one

in particular. "They need special *clothes* to make them popular!"

His sister continued to ignore him. Ma looked distressed. "Tzirel, I went to a lot of trouble to pick out something that I thought you'd like. I'll return this, if you don't want it — but I don't know if I'll have the time to go shopping again soon."

"I don't mind waiting," Tzirel said, "for the right outfit."

"Why does a designer label mean so much to you?" her mother asked. "As long as something is suitable and looks nice on you, what difference does it make?"

"It matters to *me*," Tzirel said stubbornly.

"The girls in your class won't even know the difference," Shloimy declared.

Tzirel threw him a look that said she wished he would just go away. "Oh, they'll know the difference, all right," she answered. "That's the first thing they'll notice .... Ma, *can* I have a designer outfit? Please?"

Mrs. Weissman hesitated. "I'll talk it over with your father."

"Thanks!" Tzirel seemed to take her mother's answer as a "yes."

"Don't thank me yet," Ma said grimly. "I think I know just how Tatty's going to feel about this ...."

She was right. Mr. Weissman thought the whole

idea of paying an exorbitant amount of money for the privilege of having a cute little logo on an article of clothing was the silliest thing he'd ever heard of. And he told his wife so, in no uncertain terms.

"Would you mind telling Tzirel that?" she asked. "She's going to be so upset."

But Ta was on his way out to his *shiur*. "You tell her," he urged. "I'm sure you'll handle it just fine." Praying that he was right, Ma went upstairs to break the news to her daughter.

Tzirel took it hard — as her mother had known she would. She argued and pleaded and sulked, but the decision had been made.

So Tzirel made a decision of her own. "If I earn the money myself — *then* can I buy the kind of outfit I want?"

Ma hesitated. "As long as it's suitable, I don't see why not."

"How are you planning to earn that much money?" Shloimy asked. Once again, he'd managed to be in the right place at the right time — or, from Tzirel's point of view, just the opposite.

"Babysitting," she said. "I'm going to knock on all the neighbors' doors, offering fine service and good rates."

"That's demonstrating an admirable work ethic," Ma said.

Tzirel looked confused. "What?"

"You're willing to work hard to achieve your goal," Ma explained.

"She'll work like a slave," Shloimy predicted, "and then blow all that money on some dumb clothes." He shook his head. "Girls!"

"Not dumb," Tzirel told him, eyes shining. "Designer."

Shloimy shrugged. "Same thing."

Tzirel began her campaign the very next day. She started with Mrs. Feingold, who lived right next door but had never yet hired Tzirel to babysit for her children.

"Aren't you a little young?" she asked doubtfully, when Tzirel presented her case.

"Twelve years old last month," Tzirel said proudly. "And I'm the oldest in my family, so I have *tons* of experience with kids. How about letting me babysit for half-price the first time, just to prove I can handle the job?"

That was an offer Mrs. Feingold found hard to refuse.

"All right," she said. "How does tomorrow night sound?"

It sounded perfect.

Tzirel appeared for work the next day armed with determination and a bagful of prizes for the Feingold kids. The hours flew by. Mrs. Feingold came home to find a beaming trio of children showing off their prizes.

"Well! I've never seen them so happy with a babysitter before," Mrs. Feingold said. "You're hired, Tzirel. One evening a week, and every other Sunday afternoon ..."

Tzirel went home wreathed in smiles. Carefully, she placed the money she'd earned in her old, threadbare wallet. She was on her way.

•◎•◎•

The Feingold job gave Tzirel's campaign the boost it needed. Mrs. Feingold was happy to recommend her to other neighbors. Tzirel offered each of them a one-time trial at half-price. Once she'd proved herself capable, she was flooded with babysitting jobs.

One Sunday, her friends called to invite her to get together. "We're going for some pizza and ice cream, and maybe do some window-shopping," Raizy said. "Want to join us?"

"I'd love to," Tzirel said. "But I can't. I'm hoping to do some *real* shopping ... as soon as I've saved up

enough money. I'll be babysitting this afternoon — *and* this evening."

"Don't you think you're overdoing it just a little?" Raizy asked. "We've hardly seen you since you started this babysitting thing."

"I know. I really wish I could .... But if I just keep going at this rate for a few more weeks, I'll have enough to buy the outfit of my dreams."

"With a designer label, of course?"

Tzirel smiled. "Of course."

Week after week, she stuck to her program. When her mother offered to take her to a high-school production one night, Tzirel regretfully declined; she had a babysitting job. Another evening, when her aunt wanted to take Tzirel and her cousin out to dinner, the answer was the same. And her friends had almost forgotten what she looked like out of her school uniform, because Tzirel was booked up solid with babysitting jobs every single Sunday.

If you think all this was easy for Tzirel — you'd be wrong. She'd have loved to see a play and go out to dinner and spend time with her friends. But whenever she found herself weakening, she closed her eyes and pictured the outfit she planned to buy when she'd saved up enough money. She'd seen it in the store and had already marked it down as her own. The style was right, the color was right — and the little designer logo in the front was the most right of all ….

That logo, and the label that went with it, would be her key into the world of the popular girls. Right now, they inhabited a world where she had no part. She could only stand on the outside, looking wistfully in. But all that was about to change.

When she started dressing right, she would join that exclusive club. She would be a somebody.

She would finally fit in.

And then … it was here. The big day. At long last, Tzirel's threadbare old wallet held enough cash to purchase the outfit she'd been waiting for.

She'd already shown it to her mother and received the green light. Her father scoffed at the idea of spending so much hard-earned money for a single outfit, but he'd agreed to let Tzirel buy it with her own money, and he stood by his word. With a heart lighter than a balloon, Tzirel set off for the store. It was a Friday afternoon, and she looked forward to wearing her new outfit that Shabbos — more than she remembered looking forward to anything in a long time.

The weather was not in tune with her mood. Gray and overcast, the sky had started the day by threatening rain, and was quick to follow through on its threat. Tzirel was only halfway to the store when fat raindrops began to pelt her head and shoulders. Quickly, she put up her umbrella and continued on her way.

In the store, she tried on "her" outfit one more time, just to make sure. Yes. It was perfect. When she wore it, she would look just the way she wanted to look: like one of the girls who counted.

The saleslady put her purchase in a bright yellow bag and rang up the total. Proudly, Tzirel handed over her money and accepted the receipt. Then, holding the bag tightly in one hand and her umbrella in the other, she stepped outside.

Instantly, she was deluged by a spray of rain that sneaked in under the umbrella, borne on the mischievous wind. She began to hurry down the block, eager to get home where it was warm and dry. She would hang up her new outfit in her closet, basking in the knowledge that it would be waiting for her there whenever she cared to open the closet door ....

SCRE-E-EECH! Lost in her daydreams, Tzirel had stepped off the curb without bothering to peer through the rain at what might be coming her way. Unfortunately, what was coming her way was an enormous truck.

With a gasp, she leaped back just in time. The truck

passed her with a sound like a roaring beast. The heavy rain, and the exhaust fumes billowing from the truck's rear, blinded her for a minute.

When she could see again, the first thing she thought was, *Baruch Hashem! That was close.*

The second thing was, *Oh, no! Where's my bag?*

In her leap to safety, she'd dropped both her umbrella and the bag she'd been carrying. The bag containing her brand-new designer outfit …

Her eyes swept the curb, where a river of water ran gurgling down to the drain at the corner. She spotted the umbrella first, lying mangled and sodden, like a bird with broken wings. But she didn't care about that. It was the bag she wanted. The bag …

There! A splotch of yellow caught her eye. Tzirel followed it down the street, to where the current of rainwater had carried the bag. Stooping gingerly to avoid getting completely soaked, she reached out and scooped it up.

The bag was not in shreds … but it came close. There was a huge rip right down the front, passing from the handle down through the shop's name in the middle. The skirt was still inside, but the top had fallen out. When she managed to retrieve it from the rushing, dirty water, she found a similar rip right through the middle. As for the skirt, it was a crumpled, soggy mess.

And, as if to add insult to injury, there was a big, black tire mark right across the front of it.

The truck had not managed to hurt Tzirel, *baruch Hashem*. But it *had* damaged her precious outfit … irretrievably.

There was no way to undo this kind of damage. The fine material she'd so admired was ripped beyond repair. The filthy tire mark would never come out — and even if it did, what was the use of a top without the skirt to match?

All in all, a dead loss.

As she stared down at the remains of the clothes she'd worked so hard and long to make her own, Tzirel felt as if something had really died. Tears welled up in her eyes, mingling with the rainwater that streamed down her unprotected face. As she resumed her interrupted walk home, she could hardly see where she was going. And she didn't even care.

She didn't care about anything anymore.

"Tzirel!" Ma exclaimed, as the bedraggled girl came slowly through the front door along with a gust of wind and a quart or two of rainwater. "What happened to you?"

"I jumped away from a truck. My bag fell. My outfit

was ruined." Tzirel gave the ghost of a grin — a ghastly thing that held no amusement at all. "End of story."

With that, she took off her raincoat, hung it up to dry, and disappeared into her room to mourn.

As the hours went by, Ma tried to comfort her. Ta, when he came home, did the same. Her younger brothers — all except for Shloimy — tiptoed around the house with big eyes, respectful of Tzirel's grief even if they didn't really understand it. Shloimy was the only one who had no patience with his sister.

"It's just a crummy old dress," he muttered. "Is that worth crying over?"

But Tzirel didn't want to do anything *but* cry. Ma quietly did her daughter's *erev Shabbos* chores for her, but Tzirel didn't even seem to notice. It wasn't until Ta and the boys came home from shul that night and the family sat down to the festive *seudah* that Tzirel deigned to emerge from her room. Her eyes were reddened and her expression one of deepest gloom.

Shloimy tried to cheer her up by decorating her plate with a picture he'd cut out of a magazine. It was a picture of a sad-looking clown with an enormous nose. Underneath were the words, "Smile! It could be worse …."

Tzirel didn't think this was funny at all. "Keep your silly pictures to yourself!" she snapped, throwing it back at Shloimy.

Her brother's face darkened. "Now she's going to be down in the dumps and feeling sorry for herself for who knows how long — all because of some dumb old clothes." He glared at his sister. "You don't need a designer outfit, Tzirel. What you need is a designer personality!"

Mrs. Weissman opened her mouth … and then closed it again. She exchanged a meaningful look with her husband.

Without meaning to, their Shloimy had hit the problem right on the head.

"It's not that clothes aren't important," Ma told Tzirel gently, as she perched at the edge of her daughter's bed later that night. "For a girl your age, it's only natural for you to want to look and feel your best." She drew a breath and plunged on. "The problem is that clothes mean something more to you than they're supposed to mean. You seem to think that wearing the right kind of outfit will turn you into the kind of person you want to be."

A vigorous nod of Tzirel's head told her that she'd got it right.

"That's wrong," Ma said firmly. "The only thing that will make you the kind of person you want to be …

is the kind of person you work on becoming. On the inside."

Tzirel felt her eyes well up again. They'd been doing so frequently, all afternoon. Bleakly, she wondered if she'd *ever* be able to stop crying ....

"Styles come and go," Ma said. "Fashions change. Clothes are outgrown. But a designer *personality* — that's something you get to keep. That's what lasts. And it's what counts."

For the first time since her mother had walked into her room, Tzirel started listening.

"If you go out there wearing the right kind of character — it won't matter what kind of clothes are on your back," Ma said. "Because outfits come and go ... but good *middos* are forever."

She leaned down and kissed her daughter good night. "You've had a rough day. Get some sleep now ...."

Tzirel didn't go to sleep. She was too busy thinking over what her mother had said. A million questions buzzed around her brain.

Did she really want to spend the rest of her school years — and maybe long after — working like a slave to earn money for clothes that somebody else said she just *had* to wear?

Would a designer label *really* make her popular?

And what *was* popularity, anyway? Would having

it make her any happier than she already was with her own good friends? Raizy and Shana and Hindy were the best. Did she really need anything else?

She had no answers. But somewhere deep down, she knew that just asking the questions was a good thing. Her mother's voice kept floating through them all: "Outfits come and go … but good *middos* are forever …."

All day long, she'd been promising herself that, come Sunday, she was going to resume her money-making campaign and buy herself another designer outfit just as soon as she could.

Now, she was not so sure.

She blinked in the dark, suddenly drowsy. To her surprise, she was also calmer. She was filled with the tranquility that comes after a good, long cry.

Should she start saving — and slaving — for designer clothes again, or just let the whole thing go? Right now, she was just too tired to decide.

I guess I'll give it some time, she thought sleepily. *Maybe things will be clearer in the morning …*

With that wise decision, she turned over in bed — and, in seconds, was deeply and peacefully asleep.

Braggy Berel

Nachy and his friends — Yaakov, Shea and Moish — had just started their walk home from yeshivah when Moish suddenly stiffened.

"Uh-oh," he murmured. "Here comes Berel."

Berel came running up to them, looking very pleased with himself. "So, how'd you guys do on the English essay test?" he asked breathlessly.

"Okay," Nachy said shortly. Yaakov just grunted. Shea and Moish said nothing.

"Well, *I* got the best mark in the class!" Berel beamed. "The teacher said I'm a fine writer." He fell into step beside the others. "Isn't that great?"

"Just wonderful," Yaakov said sarcastically.

Soft-hearted Shea tried to be happy for the boastful boy. "That's really nice, Berel. Congratulations."

"Yeah," Nachy said, not to be outdone. "Good job, Berel."

Moish said nothing at all. He didn't trust himself to speak.

Moish was something of a writer himself. He scribbled poems in his spare time and was usually at the top of his class when it came to writing compositions. Though Berel was in the other class and Moish hadn't been forced to hear it, Berel's report of the teacher's fulsome praise galled him even more than it irritated the others.

Nachy decided it was time to change the subject. "Guess what my uncle bought me for my birthday?" he said to the group in general. "A chess set! He's says he's going to teach me all the tricks he knows."

"I'm already a master chess player," Berel announced. "I learned how to play when I was only four. I can beat anyone in my family with my eyes closed!"

"Really?" Shea asked in amazement. "How can you see the board?"

"It's only a figure of speech," Berel told him. "What I mean is, I'm the best at chess."

"*And* at everything else," Yaakov muttered under his breath.

Still Moish said nothing. But there was plenty he *wanted* to say …

"I'm going to run for class president," Berel babbled on as he walked beside the others. "The election's in two weeks. I'll be a great president. I have the best ideas! My mother says I have a very creative mind."

Moish's annoyance increased. A nasty comment began bubbling up inside him. "Oh, really?" he began.

"Really!" Nachy interposed hastily. "Hey, guys — guess what I just remembered? We're supposed to visit the professor today!"

"We are?" Yaakov asked with a blank face. Then, at

Nachy's meaningful nudge, he repeated in a very different tone, "Oh! We *are*!"

"Who's the professor? Can I come, too?" Berel asked.

"Sorry, Berel," Nachy said. "Maybe next time …"

Disappointed, Berel mustered a game smile. "Well, have a good time, you guys. See you tomorrow."

"I'm sure we will," Yaakov said, again under his breath. Lately, Berel had taken to latching himself onto their group every day.

Berel went one way and the rest of the boys went another. When they were sure he was out of earshot, Nachy said to Moish, "That was close, Moish. You were about to explode back there."

"Like a volcano," Moish agreed grimly. "That kid really gets under my skin."

"Mine, too," Yaakov said. "In case you hadn't noticed."

"I don't think he *means* to be so braggy," Shea said. "He just has no idea how he comes across to other people."

"I'd like to *tell* him how he comes across," Moish said, eyes flashing.

"Calm down," Nachy urged. "Here comes the bus. Let's go!"

"You mean we're really going to the professor?" Yaakov asked in surprise.

"Why not? We haven't been to see him in a while. It'll be fun."

Nachy's friends agreed whole-heartedly. When the bus chugged up to the curb beside them, the four boys boarded it and found seats.

Professor Abeles was a *frum* scientist who lived on the other side of town. He had a lab attached to the back of his house and took a genuine pleasure in entertaining his young friends. Nachy was interested in the professor's scientific experiments. The others were more interested in the professor himself — and in his wife's delicious cookies. Their anticipation grew as the bus took them ever closer to the professor's house.

"Boys!" Professor Abeles was very glad to see them. "Come in, come in. Go on into the lab while I rustle up some refreshments in the kitchen. My wife baked some delicious cookies this morning." The professor had recently married, and he seemed proud as punch.

The cookies, when they came, *were* delicious. All four boys discovered that they were ravenously hungry. Mrs. Abeles brought a pitcher of lemonade to wash the cookies down with. She placed it on the counter amid the test tubes and Bunsen burners, while Nachy and his friends perched on tall stools nearby.

"Thank you, Mrs. Abeles," the boys chorused.

"You're most welcome." She took her leave, with a smile for her husband and a backward look at the boys that warned, "Remember — not too long!" She was very protective of the professor's valuable time.

"So, how have you all been?" the professor asked, when the door had closed behind her.

"Annoyed," Yaakov answered for all of them. "We've got a kid in our grade who brags night and day. It's driving us nuts!"

"Especially Moish," Nachy added softly. "Right?"

Moish flushed darkly, glad for the chance to air his feelings. "What kind of kid can't stop talking about himself all the time? 'I'm the best at this,' and 'I'm the best at that.' He must have an ego the size of a house!"

"A mountain would be more like it," Yaakov said.

"Now, boys," the professor said, "*I* don't know who you're talking about, but *you* do. Let's keep away from *lashon hara*, okay?"

The boys nodded, though Moish still looked sullen.

"I understand that you're upset," the professor continued. "But you have to try to see things from the other person's point of view."

"His point of view is exactly what I can't stand!" Moish exclaimed.

"I thought maybe you could help, Professor," Nachy said. "Do you have any advice for us?" He really meant, "for Moish." It was clear that Moish was suffering more deeply than any of the others from Berel's incessant bragging.

"People who boast," the professor said slowly, "often do so to make up for feelings of inadequacy. In other words, they worry that they're *less* than other people — so they talk as if they're much *more*."

Nachy nodded his head with interest. Shea looked thoughtful. Even Yaakov could see what the professor was getting at. But Moish was still angry.

"With all respect, Professor, I don't think that's logical. If someone boasts about being the greatest — he obviously believes it. Ber — uh, the kid in our grade brags about being a great writer, and great in chess, and great at who-knows-what else. And it's true. He *is* good at that stuff." Remembering their English teacher's remarks, Moish cringed.

"Knowing that he's good at something doesn't mean that he thinks he's okay," the professor said.

Moish didn't see it. Stubbornly, he shook his head.

"Excuse me a minute, boys," the professor said. "I need to check on an experiment." He hopped off his stool and went over to a remote corner of the lab, where various tubes of chemicals were bubbling busily.

Moish watched idly as the professor bent over one of them, then opened and shut a cupboard in the corner. Presently, the professor rejoined the others.

"Let me refill your glass, Moish," he offered, pouring some more ice-cold lemonade into it. "Drink up, it's hot outside."

Moish drank up. Soon it was time to leave. The professor and his wife walked them to the door. "Come again soon, boys!" the professor called. As they stepped outdoors, Moish heard him add, "What a delightful bunch."

"Not *too* soon," he heard Mrs. Abeles say. "They distract you from your work."

Moish turned his head at this — just in time to see the door close behind them.

"Well, at least the professor likes us," he sighed.

"I don't think Mrs. Abeles *dis*likes us," Shea said. "She just thinks we bother the professor too much."

"Yeah, I also heard what she said just now," Moish agreed.

Shea looked at him quizzically. "What'd she say?"

"The bus!" Yaakov shouted. The boys broke into a sprint.

They caught the bus with just seconds to spare. Breathing hard, Moish collapsed into a seat next to a middle-aged man on his way home from work. Across the aisle were a couple of women with an assortment of bags, obviously returning from a shopping spree. One of them was blond and the other a redhead.

"I hope Margie made something good for dinner," Moish's seatmate remarked. "I sure could use it. It was so busy at the office today that I worked right through lunch!"

Startled, Moish turned his head. "Excuse me?"

The man glanced at him. "What?"

"You — you said something just now. About working through lunch …"

The man stared at him, then gave an uneasy laugh. "I didn't say a word. You must be imagining things." With that, he pulled open a newspaper and buried himself in its pages.

Across the aisle, the blond woman said, "Josie sure thought she looked wonderful in that dress she just bought. I wish I could have told her how awful it made her look!"

Surprised, Moish glanced at the redhead. She didn't seem at all put out by her friend's comment. And why had the blond referred to "Josie" in the third person?

"Dorothy is such a cheapskate," he heard Josie say. "Always haggling with the salesgirls over the price of everything …"

Moish was perplexed. Neither woman seemed upset

by the other's nasty remarks. In fact, neither of them seemed to even have heard them!

But I do, Moish thought in a rising panic. Why was that?

"Oh, great. It's starting to rain. And me without my umbrella ..."

It was Moish's seatmate again. Sneaking a peek at the man, he saw him glance out the window in a disgruntled way. His mouth wasn't moving, and yet Moish could hear every word he said.

Said? No. Every word he *thought*.

To his horror, Moish realized that he could read people's minds!

•◎•◎•

How he got off the bus, he never knew. Afterwards, as his friends chatted around him before they parted ways, Moish's mind was bombarded by their thoughts:

Gosh, I'm starving. Hope Ma made meatballs and spaghetti tonight ....

All that math homework waiting for me — ugh. Maybe I can get my father to help ....

Good thing the rain stopped. We would've gotten soaked walking home ....

Moish is looking kind of green. Hope he's not coming down with anything ....

"You okay, Moish?" Nachy asked.

"F-fine," Moish managed to croak. Part of him wanted to confide in Nachy. But another, bigger part wanted to get home as fast as he could, to hide from the world and the many voices he was suddenly able to hear — without wanting to hear them in the least!

It was only in his room, with the door closed tight, that he was finally able to relax. No sound disturbed him here. He could think again — his own thoughts, not someone else's.

What was happening to him? Was he going crazy?

The professor, he thought suddenly.

He sat straight up in bed. It couldn't be a coincidence that this weird symptom started the minute they'd left his house. No — even before. He remembered the comments he'd thought he heard the professor and his wife make at the door. They'd been *thinking* those things, not saying them aloud. But Moish hadn't realized it then …

He must have put something in my drink, Moish concluded. He recalled the way the professor had been so anxious to pour him more lemonade after visiting the cupboard in his lab. But — why?

Somehow, he got through dinner without completely losing his mind. By being very, very careful and watching people's faces, he was able to separate what people were actually saying aloud from what they were only thinking. He learned that his mother was feeling very tired, so he offered to do the dishes. He "overheard" his sister wondering if she'd earned a part in the school play, but just as he was about to wish her luck, he stopped himself. As soon as he could, he dashed back to the safety of his room.

If this was how hard it was with his own family, how in the world was he going to get through the school day tomorrow?

It wasn't easy. All through their morning classes, Moish was listening on two tracks. The first was his rebbi, teaching them from the front of the room. The second track held eighteen or so voices, all of them "talking" at once ….

Gradually, he got better at sorting one track out from the other so that he didn't make any awful mistakes, like responding to something that a classmate had thought. He was desperately grateful when the recess bell rang. He couldn't wait to share this phenomenon with Nachy and the others.

"C'mere, guys," he said urgently. "I have something to tell you!"

His friends clustered around. But before Moish

could say another word, they were interrupted. "There you are, guys! So, how'd your visit to the professor go yesterday?" It was Berel.

"Fine," Nachy said, hoping he'd go away. But Berel leaned comfortably on the schoolyard fence, prepared to stay as long as they did.

"What kind of professor is he?" Berel asked.

"He's a scientist," Nachy said. "Chemistry's his specialty."

"You know, *I* could be a great chemist," Berel boasted. "I'm always mixing things up to see what happens. Once, I made the best drink you ever tasted. My mother wanted to enter it in a contest, it was so good!"

"Sounds — delicious," Nachy said weakly.

Berel turned to Moish. "So, did you get your English essay back yet? I'm curious how you did. My teacher showed *my* essay to the other English teachers. He just couldn't get over how fantastic it was!"

The familiar slow burn started in Moish's chest. Then, suddenly, he heard Berel say something else.

Moish doesn't seem to like me very much. Maybe this stuff about my essay will impress him ….

Moish looked at Berel in surprise. Before he could react, he "heard" Berel's voice again, puzzled and a little plaintive: *And it's not only Moish. Yaakov always looks at me as if I were a worm or something. I don't get it. Why doesn't anyone want to be friends with me*?

"Yes, my essay came back," Moish answered slowly. "I got an A."

"*I* got an A+!" Berel boasted. But there was a wistful note in his next words — words that only Moish could hear.

Maybe that *will make them let me hang around sometimes. They always look like they're having so much fun ....*

"V-very nice," Moish stammered. Nachy looked at him curiously. Berel looked elated.

Hey! Moish is being nice to me. I wish he'd be nice more often. I wish he'd show me some of the stuff he's written. I hear it's really good ....

Moish felt sandbagged. Everything he'd ever thought about Berel had suddenly turned — upside-down.

Berel didn't brag because he thought he was so awesome. He did it because he hoped to impress people into being his friends. Because he didn't think he could win their friendship any other way ...

"Hey, isn't that your class playing ball over there?" Yaakov asked pointedly.

He's trying to get rid of me. They always try to get rid of me. I wish they'd let me stay ....

Berel glanced across the schoolyard. "Oh, I don't feel like playing ball. I'm better than most of them anyway." *Moish has a strange look on his face. I'll bet he's about to say something else to try to get me to go ….*

Moish cleared his throat. "Berel? I was thinking that it might be fun to read each other's compositions and stuff. I have some poems at home that you might like, too."

It was hard to say who looked more thunderstruck at this — Berel, or Moish's friends.

He likes me! He does! … Does he?

"Sure!" Berel said enthusiastically. "That would be great, Moish!"

"And maybe you could give us some pointers on chess, too," Moish went on, with a meaningful glance at Nachy. "Seeing as you're so good at it."

"Oh — right! I'd love to."

Berel looked happier than Moish had ever seen him. He didn't need to read his thoughts to know that the other boy was feeling on top of the world.

•◎•◎•

"Professor?" Moish said into the phone that evening. "Can I ask you a question?"

"Yes, Moish. There was something special in your drink. It's probably starting to wear off by now, isn't it?"

"Yes — thank goodness. That wasn't easy."

"I'm sorry. It was the best I could think of at the moment. Did it help?"

"It sure did, Professor. I won't say I enjoyed the experience .... But I did get to see things from a whole different point of view."

"I'm glad to hear that. It's like I told you — people usually boast because they're feeling insecure."

"I know that now. I guess I really called to say thank you, Professor."

"You're very welcome, Moish."

"So, I was wondering ... can we come visit you again soon?"

The professor burst into the hearty laughter that his young friends loved. "Moish! You read my mind!"

The Girl in the Picture

Goldie took out her phone book and flipped through the pages until she found the name she was looking for. Carefully, she punched in the number. Three rings later, a man picked up.

"Hello, this is Goldie Stern. Can I please speak to Dina?"

"Just a minute, please." Goldie caught the faintly puzzled note in the man's voice. Dina's father obviously had no idea who she was. And why should he? It wasn't as if she were a classmate of Dina's, or even a close friend. Though the two of them, she had to admit, had clicked from the very start, and had worked well together all summer …

"Hello?"

She recognized the voice immediately. "Dina! It's Goldie. Goldie Stern … from camp?"

"Goldie!" Dina's squeal was loud and delighted. "It's so great to hear from you! How're you doing?"

"Fine, *baruch Hashem*. And you?"

The two girls chatted for a few minutes, catching up on their news. It had been six months since they'd last seen one another, as they stepped off the bus that had taken them back to the city from camp. Goldie had been the counselor of the twelve-year-old bunk, and Dina was her junior counselor.

"The reason I'm calling, Dina, is because the head counselor just let me know that there's going to be a camp reunion in two weeks."

"Really? Terrific!" Dina was excited. "I can't wait to see everyone again!"

"Can you help me make phone calls to the girls in our bunk?"

"Sure! It'll be so nice to talk to everyone …."

The girls went over details of the reunion. Dina jotted down the time and place.

"And, Dina, the head counselor wants us to prepare something," Goldie said. "We have to think of a bunk theme for the reunion, and make up a song or a skit."

Dina was eager to make plans. Goldie, older and more practical, suggested that they make their calls first. "Let's meet on Sunday, okay? We can teach the song to the girls at the reunion. It's not like color war or anything. The heads just want there to be a good *ruach* …."

"Sunday's fine for me — no problem," Dina assured her.

"Great. I'll fax you the list of names and numbers as soon as the head counselor gets it to me."

Goldie hung up. Her mind was filled with scenes and faces from camp. On impulse, she pulled out her photo album and started looking through her camp pictures.

There were zany shots, and touching shots, and

some shots that she didn't really know why she'd taken at all. On the last page, her entire bunk stood in a row, smiling rather mistily at the camera. That picture had been taken, Goldie remembered, just minutes before they'd boarded the bus for home.

She studied the photograph, silently reciting each girl's name. There was lively Aliza … athletic Frumi … Chaya Baila, with the whacky sense of humor … outspoken Shuli … Goldie smiled, relishing each name as she linked it to each face. Then she came to the last girl in the row.

The girl stood a little apart from the others. While the rest were arm-in-arm, there was a small gap between them and this girl …. What was her name again?

Goldie couldn't remember.

She frowned, straining her brain. She'd been this girl's counselor for four whole weeks! How could she possibly have forgotten her name?

But, possible or not — she had.

Her frown deepened. The head counselor would be sending her the list of names any time now. All she had to do was wait, and she'd have the name right at her fingertips.

But Goldie didn't want to wait. She snatched up the phone and pressed "Redial." A moment later, Dina's father was back on the line.

"Hi, it's Goldie again. I just called?"

"Yes, Goldie. Do you want to speak to Dina again?"

"Please …"

"Just a second."

Goldie didn't have long to wait. In practically no time, Dina's pleasant voice was in her ear again.

"Dina? Do you remember the names of all the girls in our bunk?"

"Of course I remember! How could I possibly forget?"

"That's what *I* thought … but there's one name I'm having a little trouble with. Let's go through them together, okay?"

Dina began listing the eight girls in their bunk. Shuli, Aliza, Frumi, Chaya Baila, Esti, Devori, Nechama … She stopped.

"Yes?" Goldie asked eagerly. "I remembered those, too. But who's the last one?"

She could almost *hear* Dina frowning at the other end, just as Goldie herself had been doing.

"We *did* have eight girls, right?" Dina asked.

"Yes. Her name's on the tip of my tongue, but I can't seem to catch hold of it …."

There was a silence, as counselor and junior counselor strained their recollections.

"It was a fairly common name, I think," Goldie said.

Dina made an impatient noise. "This is crazy. Why can't I remember?"

Goldie didn't want to admit it, but she was having trouble remembering more than just the girl's name. She could hardly even remember the girl herself ....

They both came up blank.

"Call me if you remember," Dina begged.

"Even if I don't, I'm going to have the list soon. I'll send it on to you," Goldie promised.

As it turned out, she didn't have to wait that long. The instant she hung up the phone, the name popped into her mind like a rabbit out of its hole. She snatched up the phone for the third time.

Thankfully, Dina herself answered this time.

"Dina, I've got it. It's Rochel!"

"That's right. Rochel ... Fish-something."

"Fishman, I think. Or was it Fishbein?"

Dina sighed. "We'll have that list soon. Problem solved."

"Right."

Goldie hung up thoughtfully. Was the problem really solved?

How was it possible that, with only eight girls in their bunk, one of them could have slipped their memories so easily? She'd been a reserved type of person, Goldie recalled now. Always staying off by herself, reading or dreaming or whatever it was she was doing. She certainly hadn't been part of the lively, laughing bunch Goldie had been in charge of. Rochel had stood at the fringes … apart … alone. And lonely?

Goldie felt a pang. As counselor, she should have noticed things like that. Why hadn't she made more of an effort to help Rochel along? She could have tried to help her make friends and have a good time. Rochel had probably had a pretty miserable four weeks — and it was partly her counselors' fault ….

She considered calling Dina back, and then decided against it. They'd be meeting on Sunday. There was time enough to discuss it then. She wanted to spend some time thinking it over first, anyway.

Goldie picked up the picture again and stared at it. Mentally, she ran through the list of names a second time, ending with … Rochel. She peered more closely at Rochel's face, as though trying to read something in it.

But the face, like a closed book, was unreadable.

Sunday saw the two counselors sitting on Goldie's back porch, ostensibly working on a theme and a song for

their camp reunion, but actually trying to work out the problem of Rochel Fish-something.

"She must have been very shy," Dina mused.

"I know. And we didn't help at all."

"It's not your fault, Goldie. Don't feel bad."

Goldie turned to look at her. "But I *do* feel bad. I feel like I could have done much more."

Suddenly, Dina brightened. "You know something? It's not too late!"

"What do you mean?"

"Let's call all the girls in the bunk and tell them to be super-friendly to Rochel at the reunion. And *we'll* be extra-nice, too. It won't make up for the summer, but at least she'll go away feeling good."

For the first time that day, Goldie smiled. "That's a great idea, Dina. Thanks!"

"Want to make the calls right now?"

Goldie did. The counselor and junior counselor divided up the list. Goldie would call Aliza, Devori, Chaya Baila and Frumi. Dina would call Shuli, Nechama and Esti. One by one, they told their former campers about the last girl in the row in Goldie's photograph. And, one by one, the girls agreed that Rochel *had* been sort of out of things in camp. She'd been quiet … alone … Lonely?

"Well, that's that. We've set the plan in motion,"

Dina announced as she hung up after the last call. Goldie had already made her share of the calls on a different phone and was waiting for her. "Next Sunday, at the reunion, we're all going to *ooze* kindness over Rochel. It'll be an experience she'll never forget!"

Goldie nodded. It wouldn't make up for the past, but it was the right thing to do. It's important to have compassion for those who are less fortunate than you are.

On Sunday, she and her junior counselor and seven of their campers would do their best to be super-nice to the eighth camper in their midst: the unfortunate Rochel.

•◎•◎•

With a flurry of hugs and excited chatter, the reunion commenced.

The twelve-year-old bunk was half a year older now, but just as happy to be together as they'd been in the summer. The raw wind blustering outdoors did nothing to chill their excitement. Goldie surveyed them fondly.

Four of them — Aliza, Frumi, Chaya Baila and Shuli — were in school together and had formed the beating heart of their bunk. The others — Esti, Nechama and Devori — were from different schools, but they'd soon learned to march to the group's tune and had fit right in. Only Rochel (what *was* her last name?) had been out of things. A group of one …

"*Shh!* Here she comes!" Dina hissed the warning to the others, who turned their heads just in time to see Rochel enter the big auditorium that the camp had rented for the occasion.

Rochel made slow progress through the crowded room, pausing now and then to nod a greeting at someone she knew. Then she was standing in front of her former bunkmates, smiling quietly. "Hi."

"HI!" chorused seven eager voices. "How ARE you, Rochel? How's your year been so far? It's SO good to see you!" One by one, the campers rushed at Rochel and hugged her like a long-lost friend. Startled, Rochel retreated a step.

"Hi, Rochel," Goldie said with her biggest smile. "Thanks for coming!"

"Rochel! It's *amazing* to see you!" Dina squealed, with another hug for the bewildered girl.

There was a rustle at the microphone. The head counselor was about to address the camp. Goldie and Dina and their bunk stopped what they were doing and settled down to listen.

But Goldie's mind was only half on the head counselor's words. She was replaying the recent scene in her mind, and she thought that it had gone well. They'd made a good start. After four hours of this treatment, Rochel would be feeling wonderful.

And that would make Goldie feel pretty wonderful, too.

Goldie and Dina taught their former campers the short song they'd composed and then waited their turn to perform it for the rest of the camp. After all the songs and skits were over, it was time for refreshments — and socializing. Goldie threw a meaningful look at Aliza, who herded her pals together to converge on Rochel.

"Come have some of this yummy cake, Rochel!"

"Want some lemonade, Rochel?"

"Rochel, I just *love* your outfit!"

As food and drink occupied the crowd, the nonstop chatter was muted to a low roar. Goldie was eating a cookie and feeling pleasantly mellow, when she suddenly became aware of someone tugging at her sleeve. She turned in surprise. It was Dina.

"Dina? What's going on?"

Dina looked confused. "I'm not sure. I just went over to my friend, who was a J.C. in a different bunk last summer. We started talking about some of our campers, and it turns out that she lives on Rochel's block.

And do you know what she told me?" Without waiting for an answer, Dina rushed on. "She told me that Rochel is G.O. president at her school this year! Can you believe it?"

Goldie *didn't* believe it. She felt as confused as Dina looked. Quiet, out-of-it Rochel, the girl they were in the process of pouring their compassion on … president of the G.O.?

That role always brought to mind a very different kind of girl. A popular student … a girl with something to say for herself … someone in the center of things. The exact opposite of "poor" Rochel …

"Are you sure she was talking about the same person?"

"Positive. Rochel Fishman. She even pointed her out to me. It's our Rochel, all right."

"I don't get it," Goldie said fretfully.

"Me, neither."

Within seconds, the news spread through their bunk. The campers were as astounded as their counselors. It was almost as if they were talking about two different girls! What did it all mean?

Predictably, almost, it was outspoken Shuli who ended up solving the mystery for them.

Shuli was not the type to brood about things. When something bothered her, she spoke up. So when the surprising news about Rochel Fishman reached her ears, her first reaction was to say something about it.

She did say something — a lot of somethings — to her friends. But that was no help, because her friends were just as puzzled over the whole thing as she was. So Shuli decided to take a daring step. She decided to go straight to the source.

"Hi, Rochel!" she exclaimed heartily, as if she hadn't been eating cake with her five minutes before. "How're you doing?"

"I'm fine," Rochel said calmly. She took a sip of her lemonade and waited to hear what Shuli would say next — because it was crystal-clear that Shuli was just *bursting* to say something.

"I heard something interesting just now," Shuli went on, trying to be subtle and missing by a mile. "About your school."

"My school?" Rochel raised an eyebrow.

"Or rather, about your position in the school …"

"My …?" Enlightenment dawned. "Oh! You mean, the fact that I'm G.O. president?"

Shuli's head bobbed up and down. Goldie, listening to the conversation from behind a broad pillar, held her breath. She didn't want to miss a word.

Rochel smiled coolly. "Well, what about it?"

"Er … We were kind of surprised, know what I mean? I mean … Um … Well … You just didn't strike us as the type?"

Rochel laughed. "Is that a question?"

"Uh …"

"Actually," Rochel said, as the smile disappeared without a trace, "I really *am* the type. At least, in school I am."

"Then why were you always so quiet in camp?"

Rochel was quiet for a long time — so long, that Goldie began to wonder if she would ever answer at all. But she did answer in the end. And what she said surprised Goldie. In fact, it stunned her.

Rochel said, "Have you ever stopped to think that maybe it wasn't *me* at all? That maybe it was … all of *you*?"

Shuli stared at her, completely nonplussed. Behind the pillar, Goldie listened avidly as Rochel explained what she meant.

"You and Aliza and Chaya Baila and Frumi were a foursome. You were friends in school and went on being friends in camp. The other girls — Devori and Esti and Nechama — realized right away that it was either join your group or be nowhere. So, they joined."

Shuli flushed. Looking extremely uncomfortable, she asked, "But why didn't *you*?"

Rochel shrugged. "Maybe I preferred my own company. At least it was wanted …."

"*We* wouldn't have minded if you hung around with us!" Shuli protested, stung.

"Maybe you wouldn't have minded. But you sure didn't make much of an effort to make me feel wanted. You never even bothered getting to know me. It was *your* way — or the highway. So, I chose the highway."

Behind the pillar, Goldie was reeling. The words kept echoing in her mind: *I chose the highway* …. *I chose the highway* ….

Dina came up to her elbow and whispered, "What's going on?" With a wave of her hand, Goldie shushed her. She wanted to hear this out to the bitter end.

Shuli was saying, "Wow. I didn't know you felt that way."

"No one did," Rochel said. "Because no one bothered to ask."

"I'm sorry." Shuli's words seemed to speak for them all.

Rochel produced a sudden grin. "Don't worry about it. It's all in the past now. I'm having a blast in school. Who remembers the summer anymore?"

"But what about next summer?"

Once again, Goldie held her breath.

"Next summer?" Rochel repeated thoughtfully. She smiled at the miserable Shuli. "Maybe next summer, we can all try again. How does that sound?"

Goldie didn't know how it sounded to Shuli. To *her*, it sounded like the most wonderful thing in the world.

They'd been trying all afternoon to be extra-nice to a girl they'd felt sorry for. Now they all knew that Rochel didn't need their pity. On the contrary, *they* were the ones to be pitied — for being so blind to what had been going on right under their noses last summer ….

They'd messed up, all of them. But as long as a person keeps on trying to grow and change — as long as *teshuvah* is possible — it's never too late to try again.

Goldie stepped out from behind her concealing pillar, with Dina trailing behind. She was determined to get it right this time.

And she was going to start right now.

The Committee That Could

"You look worried, Aharon," his father said as they drove home from shul one night.

Aharon gave him a sheepish grin. "I guess I am, a little. My rebbi put me in charge of organizing a *siyum* on the *parshah* we just finished learning in *Chumash*. I want it to be a really great *siyum*, Ta. Any ideas?"

Even in the dark, he could see that his father's face had taken on a remote look, as though his mind was far, far away. "Ta?" he tried again.

"A *siyum*?" his father repeated dreamily. "That brings me back to my own school days … and the best *siyum* I ever had."

This interested Aharon. "Tell me about it, Ta. The *siyum*. What made it so special?"

The silence stretched even longer this time. Aharon was about to say something when his father spoke at last. "What made it special was not so much what we did *at* the *siyum* — as what was done beforehand, to prepare for it."

"What do you mean?"

His father gave him a sidelong glance that held the hint of a smile. "Want to hear?"

"Sure!"

"Okay … I was just about your age then. Our rebbi decided — as yours did now, Aharon — to let the boys organize the party all by themselves. He appointed a committee of six …."

Six boys. Rabbi Nussbaum had put a lot of thought into choosing his *siyum* committee. He wanted to include students who were not usually too involved in the classroom — like shy, timid Binny, who rarely volunteered a word in class, and then only in a whisper. And Dov, the weakest student in class in terms of his schoolwork, but a shining star on any playing field.

Heshy and Chaim — unofficial rivals for the position of class leader — were both on the committee, as the rebbi hoped that working together would be good for them. Also Moishy, an average student whose sweet tooth turned every day into a party.

And, as the committee head, Rabbi Nussbaum chose Avi, an all-around solid student and a very nice boy to boot. He hoped that Avi would bring out the best in this disparate group and produce a *siyum* they could all be proud of.

At first, that didn't seem likely to happen.

The committee members, when Rebbi announced their names, registered varying degrees of horror. Two or three of them came up to the teacher afterwards to ask if they could be removed. Rebbi said no. "I know you can do a great job. The class is counting on you. Good luck!"

Avi was nervous. How was he going to get this motley crew to work together to produce anything? They didn't have much time — the *siyum* was scheduled to take place in just one week — so he called a planning meeting at his house that very afternoon.

If his fellow committee members did not exactly register horror this time, they certainly displayed reluctance. But they all promised to come.

And they did come, every one of them. But that was about all they did. By the time they left Avi's house an hour later, absolutely nothing had been accomplished.

It was a very woebegone Avi who approached the teacher's desk the next morning. The bell had not yet rung, and Rebbi was letting the boys play while he graded some papers.

"Rebbi?"

Rabbi Nussbaum looked up. "Yes, Avi? How can I help you?"

"I *do* need help, Rebbi. I called a committee meeting at my house yesterday … What a disaster!"

"What do you mean? Didn't the other boys show up?"

"Oh, they showed up, all right. But that was the

only good thing that happened. After that, nothing — and I mean nothing! — got done."

The rebbi looked puzzled. "Why not?"

"That's what I've been trying to figure out," Avi said miserably. "We talked and talked, but somehow nothing was resolved. I don't understand why."

"*Hmm*. I see." Rebbi didn't really see — not yet. But he fully intended to. "Tell you what, Avi. I want you to call another meeting today — at recess. Only, this time, I'll be listening in."

Avi was dismayed. "The kids won't want to meet then, Rebbi. They won't want to miss their recess."

"I'm going to tell them that they have no choice in the matter. This *siyum* is due to take place soon, and it's time the committee got cracking! Leave them to me."

When Rabbi Nussbaum laid down the law, it was obeyed. That recess found the six boys sitting in a hastily-formed circle of desks in their otherwise deserted classroom. None of the six looked very happy to be there. Had they known that their rebbi was just outside the partially-open door, listening to every word they said, they would have been even unhappier ....

"Okay, guys," Avi opened the proceedings. "Let's try to make things happen this time, okay? Yesterday's meeting was a total waste of time."

"And whose fault was that?" Heshy demanded, glaring at Chaim. "If Chaim hadn't kept coming up with the most ridiculous ideas …"

"Who, me?" Chaim said. "It wasn't *me* who had the crazy ideas. What about your idea of making up a song about the *parshah*, and you singing it — solo? When everyone *knows* you can't carry a tune to save your life!"

"This is not really useful, guys," Avi said desperately.

"We're missing our whole recess," Dov complained, straining to see out the window, where his classmates were engaged in what sounded like a lively game of baseball. "Let's get a move on!"

"Good idea," Avi said. "Now, we need to think of a theme for our *siyum*. Any ideas?"

Binny lifted his head and whispered, "I can draw a poster." He lowered his head again hastily, as though afraid that something would fall on it if he held it up too long.

"Great," Avi said. "But the poster has to be on the theme. Any ideas for that?"

"Theme, shmeme," Dov said impatiently, as a cheer rose up from the yard below. Someone had just scored. "The *parshah* is our theme, right? Stop wasting time! I want to have *some* recess."

"We all do." Avi was beginning to sound tired. "Well,

which part of the *parshah* should we use as our theme?"

"The only thing a party needs is good *nosh*," Moishy announced. He'd been quiet until now because his mouth had been full of chips. Now, with the bag empty, he was free to make his pronouncement.

"Of course we'll have good *nosh*," Avi agreed. "But I still think a theme would —"

"How about a *parshah* trivia contest?" Chaim broke in. "Two teams. Winner takes all."

"All of what?" Avi asked, bewildered.

Heshy said flatly, "You only want a contest because you got a great mark on the *Chumash* test. No way! I still think I should sing a solo."

"Let's have a color scheme," Moishy suggested. "We could have all our *nosh* be in two or three basic colors. Yum!"

"Color schemes are nice, but —"

Avi didn't get to finish. A ball came sailing up past their window. Dov leaped from his seat and ran to watch. "A home run!" he cried. "I wonder who hit it?" Heshy, Chaim and Moishy crowded behind him at the window.

"Guys," Avi called, "we're trying to have a meeting here!"

"I can draw a poster," Binny volunteered, and then retreated back into his shell.

"I've heard enough," Rabbi Nussbaum said, striding into the room.

There was a shocked silence. Under the rebbi's reproving eye, the boys at the window hurried back to their seats. Binny cowered in his chair in an agony of bashfulness. Avi said nothing, but looked at his rebbi with weary gratitude. This whole thing was beyond him.

Rabbi Nussbaum pulled up a chair and sat facing the boys. "Avi told me that your meeting yesterday was a failure, but he couldn't understand why. So I decided to see for myself. Sorry for the deception, but I felt it was necessary." He looked around the group, scanning each face in turn. "You've let me down, boys."

"It's all Chaim's fault!" Heshy declared. "Him and his dumb ideas."

"Heshy wants to run the whole show ..." Chaim began hotly.

"I offered to draw a poster," Binny squeaked.

"We never even got around to talking about the food," Moishy complained.

The bell rang.

"I missed my whole recess," Dov said sadly.

Rebbi stood up, looking stern. "We are going to continue this meeting at lunchtime. Bring your sandwiches and meet me here."

A silent groan went up from the committee, but no

one dared say anything out loud. Not when Rebbi had *that* look in his eye.

Lunchtime found one rebbi and six boys in the classroom, having what Rabbi Nussbaum called a "working lunch." To their surprise, however, he let the first five or so minutes pass by with nothing more than casual small talk.

Avi wondered what his rebbi had in mind. He was wondering if Rebbi would ever say *anything* about the *siyum* — when Rabbi Nussbaum suddenly put down his sandwich, sat up very straight and announced, "Har Sinai!"

"What?" at least two of the boys blurted at the same time. The others looked puzzled — and curious. What did Har Sinai have to do with anything?

"At Har Sinai," Rabbi Nussbaum said in a quieter tone, "we all stood together, shoulder to shoulder — three million or so men, women and children — to receive the Torah. An incredible moment, no?"

What was there to answer to that, except "Yes"?

"Think about it," the rebbi urged. "At that amazing moment, as lightning and thunder surrounded the mountain, and Hashem Himself was giving us His holy word — do you think someone from the tribe of Reuven was thinking about how he could one-up someone in the rival tribe of Yehudah?" He paused. "Or perhaps someone from *Shevet* Dan was dreaming up a new recipe for the *mann*?"

Binny giggled, then clapped his hand over his mouth, abashed.

"Do you think they were looking at their watches — if they'd had any — and wondering how soon they could get away?" Rabbi Nussbaum asked softly. He waited a moment before continuing, "Or do you think something else was happening — something so big, so important, that there was no room for anything else?"

The boys waited. Where was all of this leading?

"A *siyum*," the rebbi said, "is a celebration of the Torah you've learned. The same holy Torah that you received three thousand years ago, at Har Sinai. Don't you think that might call for putting aside your own goals and desires for just a little while? And maybe throwing yourself, heart and soul, into planning the best *siyum* you can? *L'kavod HaTorah* — in the Torah's honor?"

Six boys squirmed. Even Avi, who had tried his best to make the committee work, stirred uncomfortably in his seat. Rebbi's words seemed to hang in the air, like a silent accusation: "*L'kavod HaTorah* ..."

"The *Bnei Yisrael* stood at the foot of Har Sinai,

Rashi tells us, *'k'ish echad b'lev echad'* — like a single person with a single heart. Can't you boys do the same? In honor of the Torah you learn every single day?"

Rabbi Nussbaum did not wait for an answer. With an encouraging smile, he packed up the remains of his lunch and said, "Time to *bentch*, boys. I'm sure you'll have something great to report to me tomorrow. And I can't wait to hear it!"

"And did they?" Aharon asked his father eagerly.

"You bet they did," his father answered. "By the next day, they had a full program outlined for the *siyum*, complete with theme, decorations, games, prizes — and color scheme! Once they stopped thinking of themselves and started working as a team — *'k'ish echad b'lev echad'* — it all fell together." He snapped his fingers. "Like that!" He smiled reminiscently. "Best *siyum* we ever had ..."

The car pulled up in front of their house. The yellow light from the windows seemed to call out to Aharon, saying, "Welcome home." But he hung back.

"Ta ..." he said, a little shyly. "You were one of the boys, right? One of the six boys on the committee?"

His father turned off the engine. "I was. The names I used just now were not the boys' real ones."

"Well, which one were you?"

Aharon's father stepped out of the car. Then he poked his head back inside and said with a twinkle, "Wouldn't you like to know?"

Aharon *did* want to know. But he had a feeling his father wasn't going to tell him ....

Besides, right now he had work to do. He had to call the boys on his committee and make plans to make plans. If *he* had anything to say about it, this was going to be the best *siyum* ever!

Because they were going to do it together, he and his friends.

In the Torah's honor.

For Her Own Good

There's something about being a big sister that can make you want to turn other people into carbon copies of yourself. That's the conclusion I've come to after the events of last week.

Let me tell you about it, and see if you agree.

I don't know if my two teenaged sisters and I are bossier than average — but for our youngest sister, aged ten, we must have seemed like a triple whammy. If *I* wasn't telling Gila what to do, then either Mashi or Perel were sure to be. For her own good, you understand …

You'd think that Gila would resent all the advice we shot at her day and night. The funny thing is, she didn't seem to mind at all. Gila always listened with the same polite, obliging expression … and then proceeded to do exactly what she'd been doing before we'd said a word. It was maddening!

Let me use last week as an example.

"Homework?" I asked on Monday night, as I passed the dining room table where Gila sat hunched over a sheet of lined paper. Like the rest of us, Gila has a perfectly good desk in her room, but she often chooses to do her school work downstairs.

"*Mmm-hmm*," she answered, not looking up from the page. She wrote another word or two and then crossed them out.

“That doesn’t look very neat,” I commented.

“First draft,” she told me, jotting down another word.

“Oh?” I pulled up a chair beside her. “What are you writing?”

“A composition. Miss Fried said to write about a memory. It can be scary, or happy, or funny — anything.”

My eyes lit up. I adore creative writing. “How about a short story?” I suggested eagerly. “You can write the memory as if it were fiction, and make it really suspenseful. I could help you, if you want.”

Gila smiled her sweet smile, and shook her head. “I think I’ll just stick with a composition.”

“Or a poem? How about a long, interesting poem? That would be more original than a plain old composition.”

“Maybe,” Gila murmured, and bent over her paper again.

“Really, Gila,” I urged, moving my chair closer. “Let’s put our heads together and come up with a really super story or poem. Your teacher will love it!”

“*Mmm-hmm …*”

Frustrated, I got up and stalked away to register my disapproval of the way she’d refused to entertain my ideas. I could have helped her ace that writing project!

I'd tried my best to help Gila, for her own good. But would she listen?

I stole a peek over my shoulder as I stalked away, but I don't think Gila even noticed that I'd gone. She was busy writing again.

The next day at supper, Gila mentioned that her class would be playing a big Machanayim game against another class. "The game is on Thursday," Gila sighed. "I wish I didn't have to play."

"Why not?" asked Mashi, who loves games in general and Machanayim in particular. "It sounds like fun!"

Gila shrugged. "Not for me. I don't like sports much."

"Meet me after supper, and I'll give you some tips to make you a *super* player," Mashi said.

The meeting took place, although Gila did not look very enthusiastic about attending. It happened in the kitchen, over some milk and cookies, so I was able to overhear them while washing the dishes.

"So, what you do is feint," Mashi was saying. "Do you know what that means?"

Gila bit into a cookie and shook her head.

"It means pretending that you're going to throw the ball in one direction — but really throwing it in another. That way, you throw your opponent off guard. Get it?"

Gila nodded agreeably. But she spoiled the effect by adding, "Not that I ever get the ball …"

"Well, why not?" Mashi demanded. "You have to be more aggressive in the game, Gila. Here, let me tell you how …."

She went on and on, expounding on a favorite theme. She taught Gila how to throw and how to dodge. Gila listened, and munched cookies, and sipped her milk, and listened some more.

"Do you understand now?" Mashi asked at last. "If you play the way I tell you, you'll be a champ! And your team will have a much better chance of winning, too."

"Okay," Gila said, hopping off her chair. "Thanks, Mashi."

"You're welcome," Mashi said, looking satisfied. "Good luck tomorrow!"

At the kitchen door, Gila paused thoughtfully. "Maybe if I tell my teacher my foot hurts, she won't make me play …."

"Gila! I just showed you how to be a great Machanayim player! Why would you want to get out of playing?"

"I don't really like the game so much." With that, Gila slipped through the door and out of sight.

"Well!" Mashi fumed. "After all the time and energy

I just spent on that girl … You'd think she'd at least be grateful!"

"I know," I said, wiping the last dish and putting it away. "I tried to help her with her writing project for English — but would she listen to a word I told her? Forget it!"

"She doesn't deserve us," Mashi declared.

I agreed, one hundred percent.

The next afternoon, I found Gila in the kitchen, preparing to bake.

Now, Gila is only eleven and hasn't been baking that long, but she knows how to put together one or two decent cakes. I saw that she was getting ready to make one of them now.

Perel sauntered into the room. "Hi, guys!" she greeted us. "What's doing?"

"I think Gila's about to bake something," I said, starting to chop vegetables for a salad.

"What's the occasion, Gila?"

"It's my friend Chavi's birthday tomorrow. I want to bake a small cake to bring to school."

"That's nice," Perel said approvingly. "So, what kind are you planning to make?"

"Chocolate."

Perel frowned. "That's it? Just plain chocolate cake? What about frosting?"

Gila shrugged. "I don't think I'll bother with that. Plain chocolate cake will be fine. Maybe I'll put some sprinkles on top."

"Gila! What kind of friend are you, anyway?"

"What do you mean?"

Perel plopped herself down on a chair, wearing a definite "big sister" look. "A birthday cake for a good friend calls for a *special* effort. Come on, I'll find you a fantastic recipe — something that'll make Chavi sit up and take notice! A layer cake, maybe, with some yummy icing ..."

In case you haven't figured it out yet, Perel loves to bake.

"Thanks, Perel," Gila said, reaching for the flour. "But I think I'd better keep it simple."

"I'll help you! We could make a triple-layer cake ... or maybe seven layers! With thick, gooey chocolate frosting — or would you prefer a satiny beige icing? And for the filling, we could use chocolate, or jam, or nuts — or a combination of all three!" Perel was practically tasting that cake already.

Gila, meanwhile, had begun measuring flour and pouring it into her bowl. She gave Perel a sweet smile as she continued measuring and pouring her ingredients. It took Perel a few seconds to come off her cloud and realize what Gila was doing.

"I can't believe it! You haven't even *seen* my recipe yet."

"Thanks anyway, Perel," Gila said. "I'd better stick with plain old chocolate cake."

Perel stalked off, just as I'd done the day before. I went after her. Mashi was already in the living room.

"That girl!" Perel was highly disgruntled. "Here I am, offering to help her create a masterpiece for Chavi's birthday — and she's satisfied with the simplest cake in the world. Some friend *she* is." Her tone said, *And some sister.*

"I know," Mashi agreed. "Yesterday, I talked myself blue in the face trying to teach Gila how to be a better Machanayim player — but did she listen to a word I said?"

"Oh, she listens," I said. "The problem is, that's *all* she does. I urged her to do something really creative for her English project, but she just wrote the same boring old composition she was doing before. I might as well have saved my breath."

"We might as well *all* save our breaths," Mashi said. "Gila knows that we're giving her this advice for her own good. If *she* doesn't care, why should we?"

"That's right," Perel said. "Why should we care more about her life than she does?"

"We shouldn't!" I decided. "From now on, let's keep

our good advice to ourselves. Let's just see how Gila gets along without it …."

That decided, we separated to our different activities. In the kitchen, Gila continued her baking. She hadn't a clue that her big sisters had decided to teach her a lesson, and would be leaving her strictly alone from now on.

Gila didn't seem to mind a bit.

Mashi, Perel and I pointedly refrained from offering her the fruits of our wisdom all the rest of that night, but Gila seemed fine with that.

In the morning, when she chose a banana muffin for breakfast, thinking it was an apple one, I didn't say a word.

When Mashi noticed that she wasn't wearing the right kind of shoes for the big Machanayim game, she held her tongue.

And when Perel saw the modest and rather lumpy cake that Gila was planning to bring to school for her friend, all she did was smirk knowingly.

Gila either didn't notice … or didn't care. She smiled at us all as she said good bye, and went off to school. Mashi, Perel and I traipsed off in the other direction, headed for the high school.

There was a sour taste in my mouth as I walked. Something was bothering me, but I wasn't sure what it was. All I knew was that Gila was the most maddening, frustrating and stubborn little sister I'd ever been privileged to know!

And, worst of all, she didn't seem to care at all.

The first thing I noticed as I sat opposite Gila at supper was the big, purple bruise on one cheekbone.

"Gila! What happened to you?" I exclaimed, horrified.

She gave me a sheepish grin. "It happened during the Machanayim game. I forgot to duck."

"Didn't I teach you the right way to dodge a ball?" Mashi cried. Then, with a glance at me, she bit her lip and was silent.

Our mother smiled at Gila. "Anything else interesting happen today?"

Gila considered the question. "We had a math pop quiz .... And we got our compositions back from Miss Fried."

"Oh? What did you get on it?"

"B-plus."

"That's wonderful! I'd like to read it," Ma beamed.

I gave Gila a very different kind of look. "If you'd

taken my advice, you would've gotten an A+," I said darkly.

Perel shot me a warning glance, and I subsided.

"And your cake for Chavi?" she asked Gila. "How'd she like it?"

Gila shrugged. "She liked it fine. But Devori brought in some fancy cookies, so we had those at recess instead."

"I *told* you to make something fancier!" Perel burst out. Mashi and I glared at her, and she said no more.

As the meal wore on, I noticed something interesting about Gila. What I noticed is that she seemed perfectly content.

Content to get a B-plus in English.

Content to be a less than stellar Machanayim player.

Content to have her cake take a back seat to some fancy cookies.

In fact, Gila is a pretty contented kind of person — unlike her sisters. Mashi, Perel and I are always competing with others, even if it's just in our own minds. We want to be the best — if not at everything, then at least at something.

Not Gila.

"Meet me upstairs," I whispered to Mashi and Perel as we cleared the table. "Five minutes." We'd get to the dishes later. This couldn't wait.

"What is it?" Perel asked, sitting at the edge of my bed. Mashi was already perched at the other end.

I drew a deep breath. "It's like this," I said. "You know how we've been frustrated with Gila for not listening to us?"

My two sisters nodded vigorously.

"Well," I asked slowly, "why should she?"

They stared at me. "What?"

"Why should Gila have to do exactly what *we'd* want to do in her place? She's not us!"

Perel's eyes grew very round. "You mean …?"

"She's her own person. She *likes* who she is. Why should we try to change her?"

"Why?" Mashi echoed softly, as if the question was a very profound one.

"Yes, why?" I asked again. "Gila was made *b'tzelem Elokim* — in Hashem's image. *Not in ours.*"

My sisters sat very still, digesting this thought.

When we left my room a few minutes later, I think we were all a little bit different from when we'd come in. I hoped that Gila would notice the difference.

There's something about being a big sister that can make you want to turn other people into carbon copies of yourself. Which might not always be such a good idea …

That's the conclusion I've come to after the events of last week. Do you agree?

Move Over, Please

Shlomo Brown was the smartest boy in his class.

Shlomo Brown was the teacher's favorite.

Shlomo Brown was in shock.

He was in shock because his rebbi had just looked at him, and then looked at Eli Mosner, and said, "Eli, can you do me a favor? I want you to bring this note to the office."

Shlomo felt like jumping to his feet and shouting, "Hey, no fair! That's *my* job!"

But of course, it wasn't *really* his job — not officially. Shlomo had become so used to being the teacher's favorite that he'd come to look upon such things as running errands for Rebbi as his personal domain.

But that was before Eli Mosner joined their class.

Eli was smart, too. Rebbi had just singled him out for a special job that he gave only to his favorite students. In other words, Shlomo Brown was out in the cold.

And he was feeling just that — cold and miserable — as he joined his best friend, Gedalia, for lunch. "Rebbi doesn't like me anymore."

"You're crazy," Gedalia said around a mouthful of tuna fish sandwich.

"No, I'm not. You saw what Rebbi did this morning.

He picked Eli Mosner to go to the office for him. He always asks *me*!" Shlomo looked mournfully down at his own, nearly untouched sandwich. "Rebbi hates me."

Gedalia stopped eating. "Aren't you being a little ridiculous? Of course Rebbi doesn't hate you! You're his best student! What's to hate?"

"Well, maybe 'hate' is not the right word. But Rebbi definitely likes Eli Mosner better than me. He made that obvious today."

"Shlomo," Gedalia said. "Have you ever stopped to think that maybe this whole thing is not about you?"

"What do you mean?"

"Maybe it's about Eli. About his being new in our class. Maybe Rebbi's just trying to make him feel welcome."

Shlomo wasn't buying it. Shaking his head with conviction, he reached belatedly for his sandwich. The bell rang before he'd taken two bites. With a sigh, Shlomo packed the rest away, trying to ignore his growling stomach. He'd often noticed that when things start going wrong, they happen all at once. Now, on top of an aching heart, he had an empty stomach to deal with as well. How was he ever going to get through the long afternoon ahead?

After bentching, Gedalia followed his friend out of the lunchroom. He could see that Shlomo was in low spirits, but couldn't figure out how to help him see that there was absolutely no reason for him to be feeling blue.

The trouble with Shlomo, Gedalia thought — as he'd had occasion to think many times in the past — was that he was used to being singled out. Shlomo was the only boy in a family of girls. He was also the top student in their class. He was used to getting lots of attention. He was accustomed to feeling special. It was hard for him to move over and make room for someone else.

Rebbi's innocent choice of errand-boy that morning, Gedalia saw, had confused Shlomo. If he no longer stood at the center of the world, then where exactly was he?

As often happens, sadness quickly turned to anger. Shlomo spent the afternoon stewing, while a parade of teachers tried in vain to drum some math, geography and social studies into his head.

That Eli Mosner! What right did he have to step in and take away what was Shlomo's? He was not going to put with that. Not for a minute!

It wasn't long before he'd hatched a plan.

•◎•◎•

Gedalia noticed the feverish glitter in Shlomo's eyes as they walked home together at the end of the day. Shlomo told stories and cracked jokes. He made no reference at all to Eli Mosner.

Gedalia was grateful that his friend was no longer in the doldrums. Shlomo must have seen how wrong he'd been, and decided to cheer up.

Gedalia was wrong. What Shlomo had decided to do was bring Eli Mosner down.

•◎•◎•

"Hi! I'm home!" Shlomo called, as he walked into what appeared to be an empty house. *Where was everyone?*

"Ma?" he tried again. "Anyone?"

He followed his nose to the kitchen, where a crock-pot was emitting a heavenly aroma. On the table he found a note in his father's handwriting.

"*Dear Shlomo,*

"I've taken your mother to the hospital. Daven for all to go well! Malky and Dassi took the younger girls over to the Singermans' house ...."

There was more — something about the food in the crock-pot and Daddy's promise to be in touch. But Shlomo hardly took it in. He was riveted by the first line in the note. Ma was in the hospital! She was having the baby!

The next hours passed in a blur. His big sisters eventually returned home, with their little sisters in tow. Malky and Dassi dished up the stew that had been simmering in the crock-pot, and then herded seven-year-old Leah and three-year-old Chani upstairs. Shlomo heard the splash of bath water and the pleasant drone of voices reading bedtime stories.

He felt detached from the world, as though his life was in a state of suspended animation. Every fiber of his being was focused on the phone, waiting for it to ring. When would Daddy call?

He called at nine o'clock that night. Chani was asleep, but the others were wide-awake and eager to hear the good news.

Mazel tov — it's a boy! A new baby brother!

Shlomo stood transfixed. After all these years, he had a brother. This was going to take some getting used to ….

The commotion they made upon hearing the news brought Chani stumbling out of her room, rubbing her eyes. "What happened?" she called from the stairs.

"Ma had a baby boy! You're a big sister now, Chani!"

Malky and Dassi linked hands and began dancing joyously around the living room.

Leah stood by with an ear-to-ear grin, until her older sisters grabbed her hand and pulled her into their circle. Shlomo stood by and watched, beaming for all he was worth.

And little Chani burst into tears.

"Poor thing. She must be overtired," Malky said, scooping her up and carrying her off to bed.

Shlomo was so elated by the events of the night that he'd almost forgotten what had happened that day. He remembered it later, though. Again, he went over his plan. It was a good one. He hoped it would do the trick.

Just to make sure, he spent an hour or two at his desk, getting ready for tomorrow.

As it turned out, Shlomo had to postpone his plan for a couple of days.

The next morning, Rebbi gave them a pop quiz in Gemara, and then spent the rest of the period reviewing the answers. And the day after there was an assembly that took up part of their learning time. It wasn't until the third day that Shlomo had his chance.

He was feeling a little groggy. His sleep had been sketchy the night before, due to his new baby brother, who had just come home from the hospital with their mother, and who seemed to possess a very robust set of lungs, *baruch Hashem*!

"Rebbi, can we play Torah Trivia today?" Shlomo asked right after attendance was called.

Rebbi didn't really like the name — after all, *nothing* about the Torah is trivial! — but that was what his boys had fallen into the habit of calling the game. Usually, they played it when they'd been behaving exceptionally well and covered more material than Rebbi had anticipated. On the other hand, it had been a while since they'd enjoyed the game, and it was a dismal, rainy day that could use a little brightening up.

"All right," Rebbi agreed. "Just for twenty minutes — after we learn."

Gedalia shot Shlomo a curious look. His friend wore an excited expression, like a fizzy drink about to burst over the top of the glass. What was going on?

What was going on, he discovered when the *shiur* was over and the game began, was that Shlomo Brown was determined to outshine the rest of the class, in general — and Eli Mosner, in particular.

"That's the correct answer, Eli!" Rebbi announced. "Now, who can answer this one ...?"

It was Shlomo who answered the next one — and the next, and the next. Then Eli chimed in again with another two right answers. The rest of the class gradually subsided, realizing that the game had boiled down to a contest between two boys: Shlomo and Eli.

Shlomo felt his palms sweating as the tension increased. His usually clear mind was clouded by both tiredness and worry: *What if I don't win*? So when the rebbi threw him a question that he *knew* he knew — the answer just wouldn't come.

"Eli?" Rebbi asked.

Eli offered an answer. The right one.

"And the winner is … Eli Mosner!"

Gedalia looked for Shlomo after school, but there was no sign of him. Nor had Shlomo been around at lunch, or at any of their recess breaks. He was avoiding his best friend, and Gedalia understood why. Shlomo, the undefeated champ, had been defeated. He was embarrassed and confused. And so, he'd gone into hiding.

Of course, Shlomo wasn't *literally* hiding. He was just keeping out of the way of people who might offer a heedless remark about the morning's fiasco. And since his whole class fell into that category, he was busy avoiding just about everybody. Even Gedalia.

In a way, Gedalia's sympathy would be even harder to take than the other kids' thoughtless comments ….

Walking through his own front door at the end of

that endless day, Shlomo's shoulders sagged. He *felt* defeated — and not only in the Torah Trivia contest. He felt defeated by life. That's a pretty tough thing for an eleven-year-old to feel.

As if to reflect his mood, he heard the sound of soft sobbing. Looking around, he discovered three-year-old Chani snuffling behind the sofa. He stooped down to see her better. "What're you doing back there, Chani?"

"Duthing," she answered in a voice clogged with tears. "Go away."

Shlomo didn't go away. He sat down on the floor beside her, as close to his little sister as he could get without actually crawling behind the sofa, too. "Tell me why you're crying."

"I'b *dot* crying!"

He hid a smile. "Sure you are. I can always tell." He peered at her. "Your face is wet, for one thing." He paused. "Or maybe you dipped your head in the sink?"

That elicited a wan smile, followed by a prolonged sniff. In a sad, small voice, she said, "Mommy doesn't love me anymore."

"That's ridiculous!" Shlomo declared, sitting up. "Whatever gave you an idea like that?"

"She holds the baby all the time. She loves *him* more than *me*."

Shlomo looked into the little girl's damp eyes and felt his heart lurch with compassion. "Chani, that's just not true. You *know* it's not true!"

Chani shook her head, making the curls swing around her woebegone face. "It *is* true. She hugs the baby, and sings to him, and holds him. That means she doesn't love *me* anymore."

"Chani," Shlomo said, exasperated. "This is not about *you*!"

Suddenly, he heard the same words inside his head — spoken in another voice. Gedalia's voice. He listened to their echo for a moment, and then uttered a soft, "Oops ..."

"What?" Chani asked, her misery momentarily swallowed up by her curiosity.

He almost said, "Nothing," then thought the better of it.

"Even big kids like me can make that mistake," he told her. "Thinking that someone doesn't like you anymore — just because he's being nice to someone else."

"Really?" Her eyes were wide. In Chani's book, Shlomo *never* made mistakes.

"Really. I thought that myself ... and not so long ago, either ... about a new boy in my class. My rebbi was being extra nice to him, and I made the same mistake that you made just now. But you know what?"

"What?" Chani asked.

"I was wrong."

He saw some of the tightness in the little girl's face relax. Without planning to, Shlomo had said just the right thing.

•◎•◎•

When Eli Mosner was absent a few days later, Shlomo offered to bring his homework over after school. Gedalia walked with him.

"Aiding and abetting the enemy?" he asked with a grin.

"Oh, come on," Shlomo said. "Eli's no enemy."

"*I* know that," Gedalia retorted. "I'm glad to see that you do, too."

"He's just … the competition." Shlomo glanced sideways at Gedalia, hesitated, and then said, "Or maybe, not even that?"

"Right!"

Shlomo dug him ironically in the ribs. "Aren't I lucky to have you to set me straight."

"You sure are," Gedalia agreed. He pointed. "We turn left here, Shlomo. That's Eli's house up ahead." As they made the turn, he added, "Boy, are you *ever* lucky you have me around!"

Having a really smart kid for a best friend isn't always easy. It wasn't often that Gedalia found himself knowing more than Shlomo.

He wanted to relish every minute.

The Uglies

Esti sneaked a peek at herself in the mirror, and then looked quickly away. "Oooh!" It was worse than she'd thought.

"What's the matter?" her brother Baruch asked as he passed through the room. "You look like you just saw a monster."

"Close enough," Esti muttered. She waited pointedly for her brother to leave. With a shrug, he did.

Slowly, almost against her will, Esti walked back to the mirror and studied her unsmiling reflection. Then she offered a tentative smile.

"Aargh!" It was awful. There was no other word to describe it. Except, perhaps, horrific.

Yes, that was better. Horrific.

"I look horrific," Esti declared to a select group of friends in her classroom the next day. "I didn't think getting braces would be as bad as this!"

"It's not so bad," one friend said consolingly.

"It's kind of shiny," another added.

"Who wants a shiny smile?" Esti groused. "A shiny Kiddush cup, maybe. Or a shiny toaster. But shiny *teeth*?" Dolefully, she shook her head.

Her friends were sympathetic, but Esti was not to

be comforted. How in the world was she going to get through the next two years if she winced and shuddered every time she caught sight of herself in the mirror?

There was still some time left before the bell, but she didn't feel much like being in her friends' company anymore. As the first girl in her class to get braces, she felt miserably set apart — a society of one. She went to her desk and slumped into her seat to mope.

"Join the club."

Startled, Esti realized that she was not alone anymore. Two classmates, Tova and Shira, had come over to join her. Esti looked from one to the other. "What club?"

Tova leaned in close to whisper, "Our club."

"What kind of club is it?"

It was Shira who said, "We call ourselves — the Uglies."

Esti couldn't help giggling a little at that. "And just who belongs to the club?"

"We do, of course," Tova said. "I mean, take a look at me. Did you ever see an uglier specimen in your life?"

Esti looked. Tova was the shortest girl in the class. She was so scrawny that her skirts always looked like they were on the point of falling down. Being so small and skinny made her look years younger than her classmates. To compensate, Tova wore very expensive, designer clothes that made her look as if she was a little kid who'd gotten into her big sister's wardrobe.

"And," Tova sighed, as Esti completed her scrutiny, "as if all the rest of it wasn't bad enough — my ears stick out!"

"That's nothing," Shira said. "I'm so overweight, I'm always afraid that someone will mistake me for a beach ball. Not to mention my hair … absolutely frizz city!"

"But neither of you has a mouthful of wires," Esti said. "You should be thankful for that."

"We're thankful for our club," Shira said. "You would be, too. It's very comforting."

"Join the Uglies," Tova urged. "Where it's okay to be unsightly." She sounded like she was reciting a slogan.

Esti looked from Tova to Shira, and a slow smile began to dawn. "You know, I think I will!"

The bell rang before she had a chance to ask what the club *did*. But she soon found out. The club members had regular and frequent meetings to bemoan their ugliness. When they were together, they got to *kvetch* as much as they wanted.

It was kind of fun. Instead of feeling like the odd man out — the one whom she imagined everyone felt sorry for because of how awful she looked — Esti now belonged to a group of girls who felt just like her.

Every now and then, they would share ideas about

overcoming their ugliness. Tova would show them a new outfit she'd just bought, which she hoped made her look more her age. Or Shira would determinedly go on a diet that lasted all of a day and a night. By the time she woke up on the second morning, she was usually too hungry to take it any further.

But the club's main activity remained the same: kvetching enthusiastically and at great length about how they looked.

This activity was extremely absorbing. Esti didn't realize *how* absorbing until she held a club meeting at her house one Sunday. Belatedly, she realized that her mother had been in the room with them for a full fifteen minutes before any of them even noticed she was there!

"Sorry, Ma," she said contritely. "Did you say something?"

"No," Ma said. "I was too busy listening." There was a small frown between her eyes, as though she hadn't much liked what she'd heard.

"We're having a club meeting," Esti said. She waited politely for her mother to say what was on her mind. But Ma said nothing for a while. She just looked at the three of them, wearing an expression that said she had something to say that they might not like to hear.

"Forgive me for eavesdropping," Ma said finally.

"Since none of you seemed to mind speaking in front of me, I figured I had the right to listen." She crossed her arms. "So … The *Uglies*?"

Esti blushed. "It's a private club, Ma. Just to help us feel better, know what I mean?"

"All I know," Ma said, dropping into an armchair facing the three friends on the couch, "is that you girls have an enormous capacity for brooding about your looks. Don't you have anything better to do with your time?" She gazed at each of them in turn. "Apparently not," she concluded, when no one offered an answer to her question.

There was a brief silence, rather sheepish on the girls' part, and thoughtful on Esti's mother's. At last, Ma came to a decision. "This is not a healthy thing," she declared.

"What isn't?" Tova asked.

"Brooding about your supposed 'ugliness.' There's far more to life than the way you look. You girls have become entirely too self-absorbed. That means," she clarified, "that you spend far too much time thinking about yourselves. And not even about the most important part of yourselves. Only the way you look."

"Only?" Shira sighed.

"But the way we look *is* important!" Esti protested.

"Yes, it is — up to a point. But you girls have taken

it way beyond that point. And so …" Ma's face was lit by a sudden smile. "… I dare you."

The three girls waited expectantly. It was Shira who finally said, "Dare us — to do what?"

"To take my crash course in getting back on track. It's a three-week course — a three-pronged plan. And there'll be a yummy prize at the end of it."

At the word "yummy," Shira sat up. "Prize? What kind?"

"Do you girls like hot fudge sundaes?"

All of them responded with eager nods. Shira murmured dreamily, "Three weeks … three scoops of ice cream?"

Ma beamed. "You got it!"

Esti began to feel uneasy. *What have we just gotten ourselves into*? Aloud, she asked, "What do we have to do?"

"The real question," Ma said, "is what you have to *not* do. For the whole first week — starting today — you are not to look into the mirror."

"*Ever?*" Esti asked in dismay. She'd fallen into the habit of staring at her braces for at least a half hour every night, letting the sight of her reflection stoke the fires of her self-pity.

"Ever," Ma said firmly. "Next Sunday, we meet again to talk about Part Two of the plan."

•◎•◎•

It sounded like a small thing, but all three "Uglies" found it extremely difficult to live up to Ma's dare.

Every time they passed a mirror, they had to remember to resolutely turn their heads away. Every shop window was a potential pitfall. Every piece of silverware offered a tantalizing glance at their reflections. They'd never realized before just how much of the day they spent gazing at themselves instead of at the world. A disquieting thought …

Still, the Uglies continued to meet, to bemoan their appearances and wait for the difficult week to be over.

On the following Sunday, they gathered again in Esti's house. Nervously, they waited to see what the second part of Esti's mother's three-prong plan would be like.

"So! How'd it go this week?" Ma asked.

"Okay," Esti said without much enthusiasm.

"We survived," Shira said with a weak grin.

"Barely," Tova amended.

"Good. Now that you've gotten a taste of looking away from your own reflections for a while, I want you to start looking — I mean, *really* looking — at the people around you," Ma said. "You girls have been obsessing about beauty, or the lack of it. For the next week, I want you to think about a different kind of beauty."

"Meaning?" Esti asked.

"Ever hear of the expression, 'Handsome is as handsome does'? That means," Ma said, noting the blank expressions on the girls' faces, "that a person is only as beautiful as the things she does. We have to cultivate our *inner* beauty! And so …"

Esti, Tova and Shira held their breaths.

"For the next week, I want each of you to do something beautiful for somebody else, every day."

They let out their breaths. That didn't sound so bad.

"Also, no 'Uglies' meetings this week."

"No meetings!" Esti was aghast.

"And," Ma continued, "keep away from those mirrors!"

"Again?" Tova asked in dismay. She'd planned to go shopping this week. How could she try anything on without looking in the mirror?

"Yes," Ma said. "This is important. When training yourself to break a bad habit, you have to be consistent." She smiled brightly at the trio. "Keep up the good work, girls. See you next Sunday!"

"Your mother's really something," Shira remarked to Esti when Ma had left them to themselves. There was a grudging admiration in her voice.

“I know,” Esti said. She herself was torn between admiration and exasperation. Why was Ma making things so difficult for them and their perfectly harmless club?

“Just remember: hot fudge sundaes with three scoops of ice cream,” Shira said. The prospect seemed to infuse her with new strength.

“Right,” Esti said, glumly licking her braces.

It was going to be a long week.

On Sunday night, mindful of Ma’s instructions, Esti read her little sister Bina a bedtime story instead of chatting on the phone with her friends as she usually did. She was rewarded by a grateful smile and a big good-night kiss, which made the prospect of going to bed without her customary half hour mope before the mirror much more palatable.

On Monday, she took pity on a classmate who had a hard time in math and was dreading that afternoon’s big math test. Instead of enjoying her lunch break with her close friends, Esti spent it in their classroom, patiently explaining math problems. When the girl came over to her later, after the test, to tell her shyly but glowingly that she thought she’d done pretty well — thanks to *her*! — Esti knew a moment of pure joy.

"Do something beautiful for somebody." On Tuesday, she agreed to play ball with her brother Baruch in their backyard — something he was always pestering her to do, despite the fact that she never said "yes." His surprise when she agreed was so obvious that she felt a pang. It reminded her of little Bina's joyous astonishment when Esti had offered to read to her two nights before. When had she become the kind of sister whom everyone had given up expecting things from?

When had she become the kind of girl who stopped seeing that people needed her?

"You girls have become entirely too self-absorbed …."

Shaking her head to dispel the uncomfortable thought, Esti determinedly curled up to enjoy her new book. After all, she'd already done her "beautiful" deed for the day. Her duty had been done.

On Wednesday, she helped Shira with a book report she'd been struggling with for days. On Thursday, she offered to make the dessert for Shabbos because her mother looked so tired. Ma gave her a wordless hug and went off to bed. Esti felt the warmth of that hug for a long time.

On Friday, she took the baby and Bina out for a long walk, ending up in the park for a prolonged play session. Playgrounds bored her, and her feet hurt from all that walking. But when she returned home to find her mother all smiles because she'd gotten everything done for Shabbos in record time, something inside Esti expanded like a balloon. Something that felt as if it were filled with light and air. Maybe it was her heart …

Shabbos was a rainy day. The kind of day that Esti usually spent huddled in her room with a good book or — if she was lucky — a friend or two. But no one braved the elements that afternoon, so Esti was stuck with her own company.

Or … maybe not?

Remembering the week's experiences, she wandered out of her room to see what Baruch and Bina were doing. She ended up spending the afternoon playing games with them. The hours passed in lively companionship, and though Esti never got around to reading her book that Shabbos, she found she hardly minded at all.

Then came Sunday, and their meeting with Ma.

Shira and Tova reported the same kind of progress that Esti had felt when doing beautiful things for others. As Shira put it, "It made me feel as if I lost fifty pounds!"

"It made *me* feel a foot taller," Tova said softly.

Esti said nothing. What she had felt was too hard to put into words.

"Excellent!" Ma beamed. "Now, for this coming week, you're to continue with what you've been doing so far: no mirrors, and continue doing beautiful things for other people. In addition, I want you to develop your ability to see all the beauty that's around you. I want you to really *see* a flower — or a child's face — or a beautiful sunset."

"To keep our minds off the beauty that's not in us?" Shira asked wistfully.

Ma gave her a long, serious look. "To keep your mind on the beauty that *is* in you," she replied. "Inside of you, and in your actions. That's much more important than any beauty that may be there on the outside."

Esti was very quiet after Ma left. She and her fellow club members started off their meeting with the usual kvetches about their looks, but their hearts weren't in it. In the end, they played a fiercely-contested game of Scrabble and had a surprisingly good time.

"Let's do this again," Tova suggested as they put away the board and tiles.

"Great idea," Shira agreed.

As for Esti, she realized with a start of surprise that she would take a board game over bemoaning her ugliness, any day. It was getting harder and harder for her to feel that it really mattered, one way or another, whether she wore braces or not ….

Later, when her friends had gone home, Ma joined Esti in the kitchen for a snack. It was Esti who brought up the three-pronged program.

"I think it's working," she admitted.

"Good," Ma said with a smile. "Well, this is the last week. Have you seen something beautiful yet?"

Esti gazed at her mother's face — at the bright, wise eyes, at the mouth with its laugh lines on either side, at the determination and the goodness and the caring.

"I'm looking at it now," she said.

Worry Time

Coming out of his room late one night on the trail of a midnight snack, Shimshy saw something strange. His brother Sruly was positioned at the kitchen door. He wasn't going in or out. He was just standing very still, with his back to Shimshy, like a soldier on parade.

Shimshy took the steps in a rush and came up behind his brother. Sruly had his head near the swinging door that led to the kitchen. Whatever he was listening to absorbed him so fully that he didn't hear Shimshy at all.

"Hey, Sruly." For some reason, Shimshy kept his voice down to a whisper.

Sruly swung around, eyes wide and agitated. With a finger to his lips, he hissed, "*Shhh!*"

"But what — ?"

"*SHHH!*"

Shimshy shushed, and bent his head to listen, too.

In the late-night stillness, their parents' voices carried clearly to the boys' ears.

"This tea hits the spot," Mr. Perlowitz said. "The cake's delicious, too … Now, where we were?"

"We were about to discuss the boys' winter break," Mrs. Perlowitz said.

On the other side of the door, Shimshy and Sruly exchanged a significant look.

"We were planning to take them to that place in Vermont," Mrs. Perlowitz continued. "You promised to teach them how to ski."

"I know. It's a pity, but that won't be possible now. As I've been saying, we've got to tighten our belts. Besides, I can't afford to take that many days off from work. Not now …"

There was a short silence, punctuated by the ticking of the kitchen clock, sounding much louder than usual in the stillness.

"You're right," Mrs. Perlowitz said at last. She sounded regretful. "The boys will be disappointed."

"Blame it on the Recession."

"Sure. But what about their vacation?"

"I'll try to take a day off from work so we can do something as a family. It won't be Vermont, but it's the best I can do this year."

"That's all right," Mrs. Perlowitz said quickly. "They'll understand."

Shimshy and Sruly, the oldest of the seven Perlowitz brothers, did understand — only too well. So this was the meaning of their father's drawn face and puckered brow lately. "Recession." They'd heard the word, but had thought of it as some sort of outside force. They hadn't realized it was something that could creep into their own home ….

"I'm not looking forward to telling them the trip's off," Mr. Perlowitz sighed.

"I'll tell them," Mrs. Perlowitz volunteered. There was the clink of a cup in its saucer. "Want some more tea?"

"No, thanks. It's getting late. We'd better call it a night ...." Chairs scraped back against the tiled floor.

In unison, as though they'd practiced beforehand, Shimshy and Sruly melted into thin air.

Well, not exactly thin air. What they actually did was slip into the coat closet until the coast was clear.

Shimshy waited until the last echo of his parents' footsteps had disappeared up the stairs.

"This," he said, "is bad."

"I know," Sruly sighed. "No Vermont. No skiing."

"It's more than that, Sruly. Our winter break is the least of our problems. Don't you realize what's going on?"

Sruly hesitated. "Sounds like money is tight this year."

"I'll say it's tight! Did you hear how worried Daddy sounded?"

"Ma, too."

"Yes." Shimshy frowned mightily as he considered the situation. "We're the oldest. We have to help!"

Sruly asked the obvious question. "How?"

"We have to figure out a way to earn some money." Shimshy tapped a finger against his chin, a sure sign that he was thinking hard. "Let's sleep on it. Family meeting tomorrow, after school."

"Family? As in, parents included?"

"Of course not. We're trying to help them, right? So it's a secret."

"A secret," Sruly repeated, as he began to follow his brother up the stairs.

Shimshy paused to look over his shoulder at Sruly. "A dead secret," he said solemnly. "Pass it on."

•◎•◎•

"Okay," Shimshy said, facing the others like a chairman of the board about to take an important vote. "The reason I called this meeting is because —"

"Sruly told us!" seven-year-old Chaim broke in. "Are we going to be poor? Are we going to have to eat spaghetti for supper every night? Because if we do," he said nobly, "I don't mind."

"Me, neither," chorused Duvy and Leib, the twins.

Shimshy tried again. "It's not just a question of spaghetti —"

"No more chocolate?" roly-poly Mutty asked in dismay, reaching into his pocket for his stash of *nosh*. "No more chips? I'm not sure I'll survive!"

"If you'd all stop kidding around," Shimshy said sternly, "I'll explain exactly what we're going to do."

"Who's kidding?" Mutty muttered.

"The situation," Shimshy said, "is as follows. This country is in the middle of a Recession."

"My teacher told us all about it," Pinny announced proudly.

"Great. Then you know that it means there's less money around than people are used to. Which means that people have to work harder and make do with less."

"Tighten their belts," Sruly put in, remembering the phrase his father had used the night before.

"Right," said Shimshy. "Well, Daddy and Ma aren't going to be able to take us on that skiing trip to Vermont on our winter vacation."

He waited until the disappointed chorus had died down before adding, "I wanted you guys to know about it before they tell us, so you'll react the right way."

"Which way?" asked Chaim.

"Cheerfully. Supportively. *Not* the way you all reacted just now."

Shimshy paused to let this sink in. Then he continued, "Sruly and I, as the oldest two boys, are going to try to ease the financial burden around here."

"What'd he say?" Pinny whispered to Leib.

"I *said*," Shimshy repeated before Leib could answer, "that Sruly and I are going to try to get some after-school jobs to help pay for stuff. So our parents won't have to."

"What kind of jobs?" Duvy asked.

It was Sruly who answered. "Shoveling snow, maybe. And we're thinking of asking at the corner grocery — Greenberg's — to see if they need any help."

"Now, here's where the rest of you come in," Shimshy said.

The five younger Perlowitzes sat up, at attention.

"We don't want Ma or Daddy to know that we've got jobs," Shimshy explained. "We'll try to do as much as we can on Sunday afternoons, but we're going to try and find work on weekdays, too. So you guys are going to have to cover for us. Okay?"

The twins had a question apiece. Duvy's was, "Why can't they know you've got jobs?" Leib's was, "Cover for you — how?"

Shimshy addressed Duvy's query first. "How do you think our parents would feel if they knew we were working after school to help pay the bills? Not too happy, I'm sure," he went on, answering his own question. "As for how to cover for us — use your imagination! If Ma starts wondering why we're late, distract her."

"*And* do our chores for us," Sruly added.

"That's right," Shimshy said. "If it's my or Sruly's turn to set the table or take out the garbage, you guys will have to do it for us. That way, we'll be able to earn money without Ma noticing that we're away a lot."

"Do you think it'll work?" Leib asked doubtfully.

Shimshy looked grim. "It had better work. Don't you know there's a Recession on?"

•◎•◎•

Luckily for the boys' plans, it snowed heavily that week. Shimshy and Sruly were out with their shovels even before the flakes had stopped falling, knocking on neighbors' doors and offering to shovel their walks for a reasonable fee. When they'd done the rounds on their own block, they moved farther afield. Counting up their earnings that night, Shimshy was happy. They'd made a good start.

The next day, after school, Shimshy and Sruly visited Mr. Greenberg. The grocer was a tall, lean man with a sparse growth of beard on his chin and a twinkle in his gray eyes. "What can I do for you, boys?" he asked.

"Actually," Shimshy said, "we're here to see if there's anything *we* can do for *you*."

"For me?" Mr. Greenberg's eyebrows shot up.

"We were thinking about your customers who might have a hard time getting to the store in the snow," Sruly put in helpfully. "Or on very cold days."

"Elderly people," Shimshy continued. "And mothers with babies or small children. If it's hard for them to get out for their basic necessities, like milk and bread —"

"*We* could deliver their groceries for them!" Sruly finished brightly.

The grocer looked at their eager faces and scratched his head. "Sounds like a plan," he admitted. "But how will we let them know we've started a winter delivery service?"

That was no problem. Shimshy and Sruly would be happy to knock on doors and spread the word.

That decided, they discussed an hourly wage. "I won't be able to pay you much. But, don't forget, people will probably give you tips," Mr. Greenberg said.

Shimshy and Sruly hadn't forgotten. In fact, they were hoping for tips. Lots and lots of them.

After all, there was a Recession on.

Mrs. Perlowitz was puzzled.

For several days now — possibly as much as a week — she'd been aware of a difference in her household, but she hadn't been able to put her finger on just what it was.

"Pinny, can you call Shimshy down here?" she asked

her youngest, who was coloring at the kitchen table. "I'd like him to run out to the grocery for me. I need more cheese for the lasagna."

Two pink patches bloomed in Pinny's cheeks. "Um … did you say Shimshy?"

"That's what I said," his mother replied cheerfully. "Hurry, Pinny, or supper won't be ready on time."

Some five minutes later, Duvy appeared at the kitchen door. "You wanted something, Ma?"

Mrs. Perlowitz looked up from the counter, where she was assembling her lasagna. "Actually, I wanted Shimshy. I need him to go to the store for me."

"Oh, I can do that," Duvy assured her, sauntering into the kitchen.

His mother was surprised. It wasn't like Duvy to volunteer for extra chores. Besides, at nine-and-a-half, she thought him a bit too young to go out to the grocery in the dark.

"Thanks anyway," she said with a smile. "Just call Shimshy, okay?"

"Uh — Shimshy?" Duvy seemed to have become afflicted with sudden deafness.

"Yes. Or Sruly. I don't care which."

"I — I think they're both kind of busy right now," Duvy said desperately. "Are you sure I can't go instead?"

The niggling puzzlement that Mrs. Perlowitz had been feeling blossomed abruptly into full-blown suspicion.

"Never mind," she said slowly. "I'll try to reach Daddy on his way home and ask him to pick up some cheese."

"Great!" Relieved, Duvy scampered out of the kitchen and out of sight.

His mother stared unseeingly straight ahead. Come to think of it, Shimshy and Sruly hadn't been around much lately. The other boys seemed to be picking up their brothers' chores.

What were her two oldest sons keeping themselves so busy with these days?

•◎•◎•

"Thanks a lot, Mr. Greenberg!" Shimshy and Sruly glowed as they pocketed their first week's wages. They had delivered groceries to homebound customers, trudging through snow and slush to reach their destinations. But the sight of their pay — added to the tips from grateful customers — made it all worthwhile.

"How much did we earn so far?" Sruly asked as they walked home, heads down against the biting wind.

"I'll add it all up when we get home — Mr. Greenberg's money, plus tips, plus what we earned shoveling snow. It's at *least* a hundred dollars!"

Sruly gave a low, satisfied whistle. "Not bad, for just a week."

"Not bad at all. At this rate, we'll be able to give Ma and Daddy four hundred a month. At least."

"I'd love to make that five hundred," Sruly said.

"Maybe we can." Shimshy was ebullient. "Where there's a will, there's a way!"

They walked on, the wind whistling around their ears. It was Sruly who broke the silence. "I sort of didn't do my homework a couple of times this week."

"Sruly! We agreed to try and keep up with our schoolwork!"

"I did try …."

"Oh, well," Shimshy shrugged philosophically. "We'll work on that next week."

When they were nearly home, Sruly asked, "When do you want to give them the money?"

Shimshy had already thought about this. "At the end of the month. Then we can hand over a nice, big amount."

"Four hundred dollars …"

"Or maybe even five," Shimshy reminded him.

With that, they climbed the three steps to their front door and stepped inside into the warmth.

Someone was waiting for them. Two someones, in fact.

"Ma!" Shimshy blurted. "Daddy!"

"Good evening, boys," Mr. Perlowitz said. "You look a little cold."

"You should *see* it out there!" Sruly declared. "Talk about windy …!"

"Not a night for wandering around outdoors, I'd say," his father remarked. Sheepishly, the boys nodded. He turned to his wife. "Is the lasagna in the oven?"

"Yes. It needs to bake for another half hour or so."

"Perfect," Mr. Perlowitz said. "That's more than enough time."

"Time? For what?" Shimshy asked.

"For the talk we're going to have. Take off your coats, boys, and kindly step into my study …."

•◎•◎•

"So …," Mr. Perlowitz said when they were all seated in the small, book-lined room, "how's business?"

Sruly gulped. Shimshy looked sick. Mr. Perlowitz went on, "I heard the two of you have become quite the entrepreneurs!"

"Entre-what?" Sruly asked.

"It means businessmen," Shimshy said miserably.

"Right you are!" his father agreed. "So — how's business? From what your mother tells me, you've been working so hard at it that she's hardly seen you this week."

Shimshy looked up. "How did you find out?"

It was Mrs. Perlowitz who answered. "I'm afraid I put Pinny on the spot. He let the cat out of the bag."

"Pinny!" Sruly burst out. "I can't believe it!"

"Don't blame him," his mother said. "I made him tell me."

"What *I'd* like to know," Mr. Perlowitz interjected, "is why this whole thing had to be such a secret in the first place. Why the sudden urge to go to work?"

Before either of his sons could say a word, he lowered his voice and said seriously, "Your mother and I are concerned, boys. Right now, your primary focus in life should be yeshivah. Learning Torah. Getting an education. There'll be plenty of time for work later on in your lives."

"It disturbs us to see you boys being so money-hungry," Mrs. Perlowitz added in an anxious voice. "Is there a reason? Are you saving up to buy something special?"

Sruly and Shimshy exchanged a long look. By unspoken consent, Shimshy answered for both of them.

"Yes, we *are* saving up," he said slowly. "For something very special."

"For you," Sruly said, as Shimshy pulled their wages out of his pocket and held it out to his parents.

"There's more," Shimshy said, "up in our room. I

haven't counted it yet. We wanted to give the whole thing to you at the end of the month."

"We made a hundred dollars so far!" Sruly said with pride. "That means at least four hundred by the end of the month. But we're going to try to make it five …"

Belatedly, he realized that he was the only one talking. His parents were staring at him and Shimshy with a peculiar look in their eyes. Shimshy had also fallen silent, still holding out the money. When neither of his parents made a move to take it, Shimshy placed the cash on the desk.

"We just wanted to help," he said simply, "because of the Recession and all."

To his astonishment, his mother had tears in her eyes. "Recession! And here we were, worried that you boys were running after money for yourselves …"

"Why do you think we need your money?" Mr. Perlowitz asked his sons.

"We, uh, overheard you talking the other night," Sruly admitted. "About tightening our belts."

His father leaned back in his chair. "Thanks for the good intentions, boys. But, *baruch Hashem*, I think your mother and I are still able to manage without our children's help …. So, how did you earn this money?"

Shimshy and Sruly took turns describing their

week's efforts.

"Home deliveries, eh?" Mr. Perlowitz said with a chuckle. "Very enterprising! But I think we'll confine those deliveries to Sundays from now on. You boys need to keep up with your schoolwork. Not to mention helping around the house. Your brothers can't cover for you forever, you know."

The boys had the grace to look shamefaced. Sruly was thinking about the homework assignments he'd been neglecting, and Shimshy was remembering his guilty pleasure at avoiding his usual household chores.

"So — we don't have to worry about being poor?" Sruly asked.

"*Baruch Hashem*, we have enough. It's the luxuries that'll have to go this year — not the necessities." Mr. Perlowitz smiled at his sons. "Looks like all of us were worrying needlessly."

"When you love someone, you worry about them," Mrs. Perlowitz said softly.

There was a rustle at the door. "Come in!" Mr. Perlowitz boomed.

The knob turned and Mutty's sheepish face peeked in. "Hi, everyone. I didn't want to disturb you. It's just that I'm a little worried ...."

To his astonishment, everyone in the room burst into laughter. "What'd I say?" he demanded.

"N-nothing," Shimshy giggled.

"So," Mr. Perlowitz said, "what are *you* worried about, Mutty?"

The roly-poly boy turned to his mother and said plaintively, "I've been waiting and waiting, Ma. Aren't we *ever* going to have supper?"

Uncertainty

I signaled frantically to my friend Ruthie, who was enjoying a leisurely chat with a couple of other girls. At last, she detached herself and came ambling my way.

"*Finally!*" I burst out. "I thought you'd never get here!"

"Where's the fire?" Ruthie asked mildly.

I grabbed her arm and practically dragged her out of the others' earshot. "Guess who just moved in next door to me?" I hissed.

"Who?"

"Hinda Chaimowitz!"

Ruthie looked interested at this. "As in — Hinda Chaimowitz, the senior?"

"Exactly."

"Hinda moved onto your block?"

"She moved *next door*! Can you believe it?"

I could hardly believe it myself. Of all the people in the world who might have bought the house next door, who could have imagined that it would be Hinda Chaimowitz — the absolutely most popular girl in the school? After months of seeing the "For Sale" sign on the lawn and wondering who would finally move in, I was in total shock — not to mention seventh heaven — to learn who my new next-door neighbor was.

"How do you know?" Ruthie asked as we started the walk home from school. Usually, my backpack feels as if it's filled with bricks. Today I hardly felt it at all.

"I saw the moving truck yesterday morning. The move took most of Sunday morning, and in the afternoon I went away with my family and didn't get back till late. My mother mentioned that a family named Chaimowitz had moved in, so I kept my eyes open this morning when I went to school. I *thought* I saw Hinda, but I wasn't sure. All day long, I wanted to ask her about it, but I couldn't get up the nerve …. Finally, while I was waiting for you just now, I found the courage to go over to her. And — it's true! Hinda Chaimowitz is my new next-door neighbor!"

Out of breath from this long speech, I lapsed into a happy silence that was only broken when it came time to say good-bye to Ruthie at her corner. She promised to call me to discuss the exciting new development. I continued down the block on my own — alone with my rosy dreams.

With Hinda Chaimowitz right next door, all sorts of possibilities rose up in my imagination. Every magical door stood open in front of me. I pictured myself on the friendliest of terms with the golden girl whom everyone in school longed to be close to. I'd be in and out of her house constantly — and she in mine.

Hinda would stop me in the halls to say hello and to share a private joke. I'd stroll casually over at lunchtime to offer her some of the homemade cookies we'd baked together …. Never mind that I was three years younger — a mere freshman to her dazzling senior. Never mind that, so far, Hinda was virtually unaware of my existence.

None of that mattered. We were next-door neighbors now. The world was mine.

"I baked a pie to welcome our new neighbors," Ma remarked that evening. "I'm planning to bring it over right after supper. Anyone want to join me?"

I volunteered so fast it made my head spin. Ma's eyebrows lifted in surprise.

"I know one of the girls," I explained, blushing furiously. Though this was not strictly true — yet — after today it would be.

My little sister Lana decided to tag along. The two of us flanked our mother like a pair of guards as she rang the Chaimowitzes' doorbell.

A moment later, the door was opened … by Hinda.

I stood glassy-eyed as my mother introduced us.

"… my daughter, Nessie, who's a freshman in Bais

Yaakov. And this is my younger daughter, Lana. She's in sixth grade."

"Nice to meet you," Hinda said. "Just a second while I get my mother ..."

She disappeared into the kitchen, to reappear a moment later with a woman who looked like an older version of herself. Mrs. Chaimowitz made a big fuss over the pie, thanking Ma profusely and inviting her inside.

"Oh, I wouldn't do that to you on the day after you've moved in," Ma laughed. "But I *would* like to invite you and your family to join us for a Shabbos meal."

My heart launched into a high-speed tap dance. I peeked over at Hinda, whose expression did not change at the invitation — or at her mother's acceptance. Well, what had I expected? That she would jump for joy? She didn't even know me yet. And she was a *senior* ...

The important thing was that they were coming. I floated home on a cloud, hardly aware of my mother and sister beside me. The moment I reached my room, I called Ruthie to share the excitement.

She sounded pretty excited herself. "That's great!" she said. "Nessie, I have some news, too. My sister started *shidduchim* tonight!"

"Wow. Her very first date?"

"Yep. You should have seen how nervous she was.

But she looked so beautiful. I managed to get a look at the boy — he seemed nice …."

Ruthie went on talking. But, fascinating as the topic was, I found my attention wandering.

"Maybe I should offer to help cook the meal," I mused aloud, unaware that I'd just interrupted Ruthie in mid-sentence. "I could make the dessert. Just to get her attention, you know?"

"Sounds like a plan," Ruthie said agreeably. The nice thing about Ruthie is that she hardly ever takes offense.

I carried on in this vein for a considerable time, trying to decide what kind of dessert to make. "It has to be fancy enough to impress Hinda, but not so fancy that it flops. What do you think?"

What Ruthie thought I didn't get to hear, as her mother needed her to get off the phone. I continued the conversation in my head, debating the pros and cons of various delectable concoctions until *my* mother told me to go to bed.

That night, I dreamed I was rowing a boat made of lace cookies through a chocolate mousse sea. I woke up feeling slightly queasy, though whether that was an after-effect of my dream or the prospect of seeing Hinda again in school that day, I wasn't sure.

Now that we'd been formally introduced, I was eager to further my acquaintance with Hinda Chaimowitz.

This wasn't easy. I hadn't realized just how far apart the worlds of freshmen and seniors really were. I told myself to be patient. Sooner or later, I was bound to run into her ....

It happened just as school was letting out. As I waited for Ruthie by the big front doors, Hinda emerged through them. As usual, she was surrounded by her friends. Without stopping to think, I found myself cutting a swath through the group like a bee zeroing in on a pot of honey.

"Hinda!"

She turned. I saw the question in her eyes, and then the refocusing as she recognized me. "Oh! You're my new neighbor ... uh ..."

"Nessie Gold," I said helpfully. I giggled. "Actually, you're *my* new neighbor."

She smiled vaguely. "Right. Well, nice seeing you ..." In a moment, she was engulfed again by a sea of seniors. But I was satisfied.

"She talked to me!" I whispered to Ruthie seconds later, as we started for home. "She didn't actually remember my name, but she recognized me. She knew that we were neighbors." I related our conversation in glowing detail.

"Well, that's a good beginning," Ruthie said faithfully, if also a little doubtfully. "Right?"

"Of course! She'll be eating at our house this Shabbos, and after that I'll be able to talk to her whenever I want. Every day!"

Ruthie looked suitably impressed.

Belatedly, I remembered her sister. "So, how'd the *shidduch* go last night?"

"It went well, I think. My sister's going to see him again in a few days."

"Are you excited?"

Ruthie gave me her unflappable smile. "It's way too early for that."

As far as I was concerned, it was never too early to build dream castles in the air. As we walked home together, Ruthie may have told me more about her sister and the boy she was seeing. Or maybe not. Truth be told, I wasn't listening all that hard. I had dream castles of my own to build.

Shabbos came at last. I was so nervous, so eager to impress Hinda, so determined to wow her with my conversation, that I became completely tongue-tied at

the table. I barely said two words to her all through the meal. Hinda acknowledged my mother's, "Nessie made the dessert," by glancing at me with a faint grin. I lived on that grin for days.

All the next week, I hovered — in the halls, in the lunchroom, by the front doors — on the off chance that I might run into Hinda. Now and then, I did. When that happened, I would dart forward to babble something to her, like a puppy eager for a pat on the head.

Sometimes, I got one. Not a pat on the head precisely, but a casually friendly remark that lifted me into the stratosphere as if I was riding a hot-air balloon.

At other times, I got nothing more than a vague nod acknowledging my existence. Hinda was always surrounded by girls her own age. She seemed to be in the center of every popular crowd. At this rate, I would never become as close to her as I longed to be.

Something would have to be done.

"I'm out of sugar," Ma said with a worried frown. "Nessie, I need you to run down to the store for me."

At once, my heart launched into its tap-dancing routine. "How much do you need?"

"Only a cup. But I need it now."

"Why don't I borrow it from the neighbors?" I held my breath.

"The Weissmans?" Ma asked skeptically. The Weissmans were an elderly couple who did not welcome visitors — especially young ones.

"No — I meant the new neighbors. The Chaimowitzes."

Ma's brow cleared. "Of course! Good thinking, Nessie. Here, take this measuring cup along. Tell Mrs. Chaimowitz I'll return the sugar tomorrow, *im yirtzeh Hashem*."

I was more than happy to tell Mrs. Chaimowitz anything at all — as long as it gave me a chance to see Hinda.

As on our first visit, it was Hinda who opened the door. Stammering in my nervousness, I held out the measuring cup and told her what I needed. While her mother measured out the sugar, Hinda engaged me in casual conversation.

I hardly remember what we said. I think she asked me which teachers I had, and I believe I held onto enough of my wits to tell her. Then I asked her what she planned to do after graduation, and she mentioned the name of a seminary I'd never heard of. How this fascinating conversation might have continued is anyone's guess; Mrs. Chaimowitz returned with the sugar much too soon.

"Well, bye," I said reluctantly.

"Bye, Nessie."

Nessie. She'd called me by my name. I was a real person to her now.

"Drop by anytime!" I said cheerily, and made my escape.

Thirty seconds later, I was on the phone with Ruthie. I gave her a blow-by-blow account of my exciting encounter with Hinda. "Do you think she likes me?" I asked eagerly.

"Oh, I'm sure she does," Ruthie said warmly. "What's not to like?"

I wasn't sure. What kind of girl *did* Hinda like? Had her friendliness come from genuine interest, or was she just being polite? I had no way of knowing for sure.

In this state of uncertainty, I finally fell asleep. I dreamed of crossroads, with arrows pointing in every direction and utterly confusing me. Not surprisingly, I awoke more tired than when I'd gone to bed.

Maybe because I was so tired, I saw things through a cloud of gray that day. I passed Hinda in the hall and waved, but she either didn't see me or pretended not to. Later, after school, she said "Hi" in response to my greeting and then turned back to her bevy of friends.

My uncertainty grew. *Were* we becoming friends, or

was all this nothing more than wishful thinking on my part?

Ruthie was sympathetic. “Come to my house,” she urged. “You haven’t been over in ages.”

This was true. I’d taken to hanging around my own backyard every evening in the hopes of catching a glimpse of Hinda going in or out. Guiltily, I agreed to Ruthie’s suggestion.

At Ruthie’s house, we found her Aunt Chaya visiting. She greeted us pleasantly enough, but it soon became clear that it was Ruthie’s sister she’d come to see. The moment we were out of the room, she resumed the talk our entrance had interrupted.

“Well?” Aunt Chaya asked.

“I’m not sure,” Ruthie’s sister said. “I wonder what he thinks of me ….”

“Right now, it doesn’t matter what *he* thinks of *you*,” Aunt Chaya said firmly. “What I want to know is, how do *you* feel? What do you like about him? You have to know your own mind!”

There was more, but we were out of range. I was thoughtful as I took a seat in Ruthie’s room and waited for her to fetch some snacks.

You have to know your own mind ….

I thought about the see-saw of uncertainty I’d been riding since Hinda Chaimowitz moved in next door.

Up one day, down the next. *Does* she like me — *doesn't* she like me? But there was one question I hadn't bothered to ask myself.

In my mind, I heard the echo of Aunt Chaya's voice. "How do *you* feel?"

You have to know your own mind ….

To do that, I had to figure out what sort of things I liked. I mean, really liked. The thrill of being on chummy terms with a senior was fun. But did that rate among my Top Ten likes?

I started figuring.

I liked the people in my family. Really liked them.

I liked reading good books.

I liked swimming in the summers.

The last two items were pretty superficial. I tried to probe more deeply.

I liked the warm feeling I got from knowing that I could pick up a phone and say anything that was on my mind to my friend at the other end.

I liked the comfortable feeling of walking together with my friend, even if we weren't saying much.

I liked knowing that I had a friend who accepted me just the way I was, and didn't turn away or take offense if I sometimes got things wrong.

As Ruthie walked back into the room bearing a tray of snacks and drinks, the words rolled around my mind as though spelled out in big, bold letters: "I like *you*!"

Ruthie must have seen something in my face. As she set down the tray, she said, "What?"

"Nothing," I said, smiling hard. "Wanna have a sleepover tonight? It's been a while."

Ruthie's face lit up. "Sure! At your house, or here?"

"Here's fine," I said. The magnet-pull of the house next door was no more. "If your mother lets."

"I'll go ask."

Ruthie's mother said a sleepover was fine, so I went home to ask my mother and collect my stuff. Afterwards, Ma walked me to the door to say good-bye. Someone came out of the house next door.

"Isn't that the Chaimowitz girl?" Ma asked, peering down the street in the gathering dusk.

I glanced at the figure walking away from us. "Yes, that's Hinda."

"Nice girl," Ma remarked.

"She sure is," I agreed.

Then, with a kiss for my mother, I hurried back to Ruthie's house. Because, nice as Hinda might be, I knew someone even nicer.

And that someone — unlike the Hinda Chaimowitzes of this world — was actually interested in being my friend!

Zalmy Takes His Medicine

"**Eli**, please take out the garbage," Mrs. Schwartz called from the kitchen.

In the living room, where he was playing Monopoly with his two younger brothers, Eli shook the dice and moved his piece five spaces ahead. "You owe me rent," he told his brother Avrumi.

"Shaya owes *me* rent!" Avrumi said. "I forgot to collect it from him last time."

"Too late," Shaya said with a complacent grin. "You should've remembered."

"Eli!" his mother called again. "The garbage!"

With a shrug, Eli got to his feet. "Work it out, you guys. I'll be back in a minute."

But Eli wasn't back in a minute — not at the board game, anyway. In about sixty seconds, he was going to have a lot more on his mind than collecting rent for an imaginary hotel on an imaginary block ….

•◎•◎•

"Okay, Ma," Eli said, walking into the kitchen. "Here I am."

"How about coming the first time I call you?" she asked, handing him two bulging trash bags.

"Sorry …"

"Go on. And close the door behind you. It's cold out there."

Using his foot to swing the door shut behind him, Eli stepped through it with his arms full of garbage.

His mother was right: It was cold. As he made his way around the side of the house, his teeth started chattering — which may explain why he didn't hear the whisper at first.

"*Psst* … Eli!"

Eli continued on toward the trash cans, moving as fast as he could. He couldn't wait to get back inside, where it was nice and warm.

"*Psst* … ELI!"

This time, the stage-whisper penetrated. Eli froze in the act of dumping his bags in the can. His head swiveled frantically around. "Who's that? Who called me?"

"It's me! Zalmy!"

"Where are you?"

"Behind the shed. Hurry — I'm freezing!"

So was Eli, but this was no time to make a point of it. Afire with curiosity, he moved toward the shed. "Where? I can't see you."

"That's because I'm *hiding*." With a cautious glance around, Zalmy stepped out from behind the shed. The two boys looked at each other for a moment.

Eli's friend was wearing a warm jacket, which was more than he could say for himself. But Zalmy's face was pinched with cold. How long had he been shivering behind the shed on this frigid night?

"What are you doing here?" Eli asked wonderingly.

"I'm in trouble. Or at least, I will be when my mother finds out … Listen, could we continue this conversation inside? I'm so cold, I can hardly talk!"

Eli nodded. "Sure. Come inside. I'll fix you a hot drink."

"I don't want your parents to see me — or they'll be on the phone in two seconds, calling *my* parents."

"But why —"

"Later, Eli. Just get me into the house first, okay?" Zalmy's teeth were chattering even louder than Eli's.

"Okay, wait here. I'll go see if the coast is clear …."

Leaving his friend skulking by the shed, Eli slipped through the back door into the blessedly warm kitchen.

There was no sign of his mother. Listening hard, he heard her voice floating faintly back to his ears from upstairs. Quickly, he rushed back outside, steeling himself against the blast of icy air that engulfed him in an instant.

"Zalmy!" he whispered loudly, waving for all he was worth. "Let's go!"

Zalmy was at his side almost before the words were

out of his mouth. He followed close on Eli's heels as they stepped into the kitchen. Eli poked his head out the kitchen door — and encountered two very impatient stares from his younger brothers.

"C'mon, Eli!" Avrumi complained. "How long does it take to get rid of some garbage?"

"We've been waiting for *ages*!" Shaya chimed in.

Eli put a warning finger to his lips. "Quiet, you guys," he said, very softly.

"What?" Shaya asked. He turned to Avrumi. "What'd he say?"

"I said QUIET!" Hastily, Eli lowered his voice. "Zalmy's here, and he doesn't want Ma or Ta to see him. Shaya, run upstairs and tell me where Ma is. Quick!"

Shaya's eyes grew very round. Without a word, he put down his Monopoly money and scooted up the stairs, quiet as a mouse.

In the living room, Avrumi was curious. "What's going on, Eli? Why is Zalmy here? Why —"

"*Shhh!* You'll hear all about it soon. First, we have to get Zalmy safely upstairs …." Eli looked up anxiously, willing Shaya to reappear.

A moment later, he did. The seven-year-old clattered down the stairs, forgetting to keep quiet this time.

"Ma's in Rina's room, telling her a bedtime story," Shaya reported.

"Good. C'mon, Zalmy. If we're very quiet, I can smuggle you into my room without anyone seeing you." Eli led the way.

They made a strange procession: Eli first, taking each step as though it were made of glass, followed by Zalmy, hunched inside his jacket as though he wished it could cover him from head to toe, with Eli's two brothers bringing up the rear like a pair of Indian scouts. Eli had just reached the upstairs landing when a sound from downstairs made his blood turn to ice. It was the sound of a key turning in the front door.

"It's my father!" he hissed. "Hurry!"

He darted down the hall, past the half-open door where his mother's gentle voice murmured to his sleepy little sister, past the bathroom, past the linen closet .... His room had never seemed so far away before. At last, he pushed open the door and flung himself inside. Zalmy, Avrumi and Shaya piled in right after him.

"Whew!" Eli closed the door and leaned against it. "When I heard my father coming in, I almost fainted .... But we made it!"

"Thank goodness." Zalmy threw himself onto the bed. "And thank goodness you came outside just now. I was never so cold in my life." He was still shivering.

Eli sat beside his friend. Avrumi took the desk chair, while Shaya arranged himself cross-legged on the rug, as though ready to hear a good story. Which, in fact, he was. "Why are you hiding, Zalmy?" he asked.

Eli threw his little brother a look that said, "Don't ask questions." A second later, he asked one of his own. "Do you need anything? Hot cocoa, maybe?"

"Not right now. It might make your mother suspicious. I don't want them to know I'm here."

"But why *not*?" Shaya begged.

"Yes," Eli said, losing patience. "Why not, Zalmy?"

Zalmy took a long, quivering breath. "Here's what happened. I was kicking a soccer ball around the living room after supper. My mother's always telling me not to do it … but I forgot." He looked so miserable that Shaya said kindly, "That's okay. I forget things, too. Lots of times."

"Thanks." Zalmy gave him a feeble grin. "Anyway, before I knew it, my soccer ball flew a little higher than I meant it to. It flew right up to the dining room table."

"Were there dishes on the table?" Eli asked, beginning to glimpse the outlines of his friend's problem.

"Worse. There was a brand-new, *gigantic* glass vase that my mother shlepped home from the store yesterday. And a bunch of humongous fake flowers to go with it. My mother's been so happy about that vase and those flowers. All day, yesterday and today, she kept saying how nicely they dress up the dining room."

Zalmy looked down at the floor. "Well, it doesn't look so dressed-up anymore …."

"What happened when the ball hit the vase?" Avrumi asked. "Didn't your mother hear?"

"She and my father are at a wedding. I threw away the pieces of glass and left the flowers on the table. Some of them are still in one piece …. And then" — Zalmy hugged his jacket more closely around him, as though it were his only friend in the world — "I ran away from home."

"Come on, Zalmy," Eli said. "You know you can't keep away forever. Sooner or later, you're going to have to go back."

"Maybe not," Zalmy said hopefully. "Maybe I can stay here. I won't take up much room. I can stay in the closet, or under the bed, or something …."

Before Eli could answer, there was a tap on the door. Like a shot, Zalmy dropped to the floor and slithered under the bed.

"Eli?" his mother called. "Is Shaya in there with you? It's almost his bedtime."

"Just a few more minutes, Ma!" Shaya called back desperately. This adventure was way too exciting to miss. "I, uh … am a little hungry. Can I have a snack first?"

"Make it quick, Shaya. It's getting late."

They listened to the sound of her footsteps retreating down the hall.

"Do you think you could get me a little something, too?" Zalmy asked plaintively. "A guy gets hungry, standing out in the cold."

"Sure," Shaya said. "What do you want?"

"Bring a bag of chips, and some pretzels," Eli instructed him. "And something to drink." He eyed his friend as if to ask, "Is that okay?" Zalmy nodded gratefully.

"And some fruit," Avrumi called as Shaya started to leave the room. "To give Zalmy energy."

"What do I need energy for?" Zalmy grumbled.

Avrumi shrugged. "If you don't eat the fruit, I will." Avrumi stood out among his brothers in his passion for healthy snacks.

Downstairs in the kitchen, Shaya was doing his best to fill the order. First, he stuffed a chip bag into his pocket. Then he tucked a bag of pretzels under one arm and some bottled water under the other. Last of all, he went to the fruit bowl on the table and started piling oranges and apples into the crook of his arm.

When everything was safely distributed in his arms and pockets, he started upstairs. From the living room, his mother called, "Five more minutes, Shaya."

"Okay, Ma." He quickened his pace.

"I'll be up to say good night soon," his father called next.

"Okay, Ta …"

At the end of the hall, he banged on the door with the tip of his shoe. "Let me in!" he whispered loudly. "My hands are full!"

Eli opened the door. No sooner did Shaya step through, then all the fruit tumbled from his grasp. *Bump, thump, thump* went the oranges and apples. Downstairs, his parents looked at each other.

"What was that?" Ta asked.

"He said he was getting a snack," Ma replied.

"That's a pretty loud snack …."

They listened, but there was no more noise from above. Still, Shaya's father lifted himself up from his chair and started for the stairs. "I'll just go check that all's well …. I wanted to say 'hi' to the boys, anyway."

The sound of Mr. Schwartz's approaching footsteps sent Zalmy into a panic. Moving like lightning, he darted over to the closet and went inside, pulling the door shut behind him. "Remember — not a word!" he pleaded just before he disappeared.

With a quick rap on the door, Eli's father came in. "Hello, boys," he said. "Having a secret conference?"

Eli looked startled; Avrumi looked guilty; Shaya

looked scared. It was Eli who said, "Uh, nothing special, Ta. We're just hanging around."

"What was that thunder I just heard coming from this room?"

"I spilled some fruit," Shaya said in a small voice.

"Oh?" His father eyed the pile of apples and oranges on the desk. "That's a lot of fruit you've got there."

"We were hungry." As if to prove his point, Avrumi grabbed an apple, made a *brachah* and took a bite.

"*Amein*," said Ta. "Shaya, isn't it past your bedtime? Come on, I'll tuck you in …."

With an agonized backward look toward his brothers and the closet, Shaya allowed himself to be led away.

When they had the room to themselves again, Avrumi tapped on the closet door. "The coast is clear, Zalmy. You can come out now."

Hesitantly, Zalmy opened the door a crack. "Are you sure?"

"Positive. Ta's putting Shaya to bed, and Ma's downstairs."

Zalmy trudged over to the bed and plopped himself down again. It must have been stuffy in the closet, because he'd finally unzipped his jacket. Absently, he opened the chip bag.

"We have to figure something out," Eli said. "You

can't hide in here forever, Zalmy. We've barely managed to keep you a secret tonight — and it's only been a half hour or so!"

"How long have you been gone?" Avrumi asked curiously.

Zalmy checked his watch. "I broke the vase at seven-twenty-eight. I was out the door by seven-thirty."

"Quick work," Eli said admiringly.

"I was terrified," Zalmy admitted. "Luckily, my big sisters were upstairs doing their homework and the little ones were already in bed." He turned pleading eyes to Eli. "Please let me stay here tonight. I don't want to go back."

"Your parents will go crazy worrying about you," Eli protested.

"You can make an anonymous call, telling them that I'm alive and well. Just don't tell them where I am."

Eli was pondering this when the sound of approaching footsteps galvanized Zalmy into action again. Like a shot, he was back in the closet. "I don't know how much more of this I can take," he whispered, just before the door shut to plunge the closet into darkness.

Eli and Avrumi's father was back. "Shaya seems very antsy tonight," he remarked.

"Oh?" Eli tried to look unconcerned.

"Yes. Have you boys been playing a scary game or anything like that?"

Both boys shook their heads.

"Telling him ghost stories, maybe?"

Another solemn head shake.

Ta was about to say something else, when from the closet came the distinct sound of a sneeze.

"*Gezuntheit*," Ta said automatically. He looked at his sons. "Now, where were we?"

"Uh … Uh …" Eli couldn't think straight. Zalmy had sneezed! And Ta had said, "*Gezuntheit*!" He signaled Avrumi frantically with his eyes, silently asking, "What do we do now?"

"Sometimes, little kids get scared from the smallest things," their father continued. "Like coming up behind them and shouting, 'Boo!' Or …" He strode casually across the room. "Jumping unexpectedly out of a dark closet …" He grasped the knob and flung open the closet door.

Ta looked down at the figure huddled on the closet floor. The figure had his eyes squeezed tightly shut, as though hoping that would make him invisible.

"Zalmy!" Ta said heartily. "Welcome to our humble abode. Please, come out. No need to be all by yourself in the dark."

Slowly, Zalmy opened his eyes. Even more slowly,

he straightened up and stepped out of the closet.

"Now ..." Ta looked at Eli, then at Avrumi, and then at Eli's friend. "I want to know what this is all about."

In halting words, with frequent interjections by Eli and Avrumi, Zalmy told him.

"I see. You broke your mother's new vase —"

"It's not just *any* vase, Mr. Schwartz. It's huge, and it cost plenty. And it wasn't easy for my mother to *shlep* it home. She just got it yesterday. And she really loved the way it looked in our dining room ..." Zalmy stopped talking as a sob rose in his throat and got in the way.

The boys' father looked very sober. "You boys made a serious mistake tonight," he said.

"It was my fault!" came a thin voice from the door. Shaya stood there in his pajamas. "I shouldn't have dropped the fruit!"

"No, it was my fault," Eli said. "I shouldn't have sent you."

"It was *my* fault for asking for fruit in the first place," Avrumi said nobly.

"Wrong — on all counts. I'm not talking about the mistake that led me to discover what was going on. That," Mr. Schwartz said with a sudden twinkle, "was a simple sneeze."

"My fault," moaned Zalmy.

"Correct," said Mr. Schwartz. "But not for sneezing.

For running away from your house — instead of staying home to face the music."

"But I couldn't!" Zalmy shuddered. "I was scared to! I'm in such hot water ...."

"All the more reason to take your medicine and get it over with," Mr. Schwartz told him. "Hashem punishes people when they do something wrong, and there's nothing wrong with parents doing the same when their children disobey. In fact, it's when there are *no* consequences that the real trouble begins ...."

Zalmy hung his head. He wasn't convinced.

"What you need to do, when you've made a mistake, is own up to it," Eli's father said. "And take your medicine like a man. I guarantee — that will make you think twice before making that same mistake again." He looked at their visitor. "So, have you learned something tonight, Zalmy?"

"Yeah," Zalmy said with a woebegone expression. "Never play soccer in the dining room again ..."

"Right. Now, I'm going to take you home, where your sisters are probably frantic by now. And when your parents come back, I want you to confess what you did and offer to pay for it out of your own money. And if your parents give you a punishment, I want you to accept it like a man — because you deserve it. Can I count on you to do that, Zalmy?"

Slowly, Zalmy nodded.

"Running away from problems never solves them," Mr. Schwartz added softly. "Trust me on that."

He sent Shaya back to bed and herded Zalmy down the stairs. After a quick word of explanation to his wife, he walked Zalmy down the block to his own house, where — as he'd predicted — his sisters had been climbing the walls with worry.

•◎•◎•

Back home again, Mr. Schwartz climbed the stairs to Eli's room. He found Avrumi still there, munching on another apple.

"So," their father said, "Zalmy's learned to take his medicine."

"I guess so," Eli mumbled.

"But what about you? You're the one who let him into the house … who hid him from your mother and me … who led this whole secret escapade. What medicine do you think *you* deserve?"

Eli looked panic-stricken. What would his punishment be? Would his parents cancel camp for the summer? Take away his new bike? Ground him for the rest of the year?

His terror showed clearly in his eyes. So did his remorse. "I'm really sorry, Ta. I know I shouldn't have done it. If — if you want to punish me, I'll … try to take it like a man. But could I pleeeeeze go to camp this summer?"

Stifling a smile, Mr. Schwartz nodded his head. Eli's panic was punishment enough for now. "If you're really sorry, then we'll let it go with a warning — this time."

"There won't *be* a next time, Ta. You can count on it," Eli said earnestly.

"I hope not. Remember, running away from a problem never solves it."

"Right!" came a small voice from the doorway.

Ta turned. "Shaya! You again?"

Shaya nodded. "I couldn't fall asleep until I found out how the adventure ended."

His father stood up and took him by the hand. "Come back to bed, and I'll tell you. It's the story of 'The Boy Who Wouldn't Take His Medicine' …."

"Did you ever tell me that story before?" Shaya asked as he pattered along the hall beside his father.

"No," Ta said with a smile. "This one is brand-new."

What's the Story?

"Ma!" Rivi cried as she burst into the kitchen. "I need a favor!"

Her mother was about to try out a new recipe. "*Hmm?*" she said absently.

"It's due tomorrow. My teacher'll *kill* me if I don't hand it in on time," Rivi continued dramatically.

"I seriously doubt that." Ma put down her cookbook. "Can it wait? I'm in the middle of something here."

"This'll only take a minute .... Okay, maybe a *little* longer. My English teacher wants us to interview one of our parents about why they chose the job or career they have. Daddy's not home ...."

"Which leaves me," Ma said, suppressing a sigh. "Oh, well. The cookies can wait, I suppose." She pulled out a chair at the kitchen table, and her daughter gratefully did the same. Rivi produced a rather dog-eared notebook and a pen, which she held poised over the page as if to say, "Ready whenever you are!"

Ma quirked an eyebrow at her. "Doesn't an interview mean that you ask me questions?"

"I *did* ask a question, Ma. I asked why you chose the job you do."

Ma laughed. "I didn't really choose it. You could say that *it* chose *me*."

"Really?"

"Really."

"You know something?" Rivi said in surprise. "You never actually told me how it all began. Why not?"

"Well, it's a little embarrassing …."

Rivi stared at her mother in amazement. "Embarrassing — how?"

"Let's just say that the early parts don't exactly show me in my best light," Ma explained.

Rivi was interested. "So, what's the story?"

Ma's eyes took on a faraway look. "It all started when I was a little kid," she began. "Probably one of the most annoying little kids you'd ever hope to meet …"

•◎•◎•

My initials are "C.B." (Ma said), and that's the nick-name my family called me by. Pretty soon, though, they decided that those initials also stood for something else. They stood for "Chatter Box"!

Yes, I was a chatterer — from the minute I learned how to talk.

I liked to share every little thing about my day with my mother. I told my father about my dreams each morning. I filled in my brothers and sisters on the events of my life as they occurred.

And I gave them all the full, unabridged version! I

included every word of every conversation. I provided details about the details. It never occurred to me that the people in my family didn't have an infinite number of hours in the day to devote to my stories. I just assumed that they were as happy to listen to me chatter as I was to do it.

I assumed wrong.

One night at supper, as I spun a long, long yarn at the table about some incident that had happened at school, my oldest brother Gavriel let out an elaborate yawn. My other brother, Shimi, made a chopping motion with his hand. "Cut it short, C.B.," he begged. "We don't have all night!"

I was surprised. *I* had all night. "I'm almost done," I promised. And on I went.

The problem was, as a little kid my constant chattering had been kind of cute. Now that I was a big girl in the sixth grade, it wasn't so cute anymore. In fact, it was downright annoying. My parents exchanged a glance and motioned for my long-suffering brothers to hear me out. My younger sisters generally had more patience for my stories, but tonight even they were getting restless. My mother sought me out after supper to give me a little advice.

"The thing is," she said as we washed and dried the dishes together, "people don't always have the time or attention to give to long drawn-out stories. Understand what I mean, C.B.?"

I didn't want to understand. "How come everyone else gets to talk, and not me?"

"Of course you can talk," my mother said patiently. "Just don't dominate the conversation. Give others a chance to get a word in edgewise. And another thing ..." She smiled. "You know what they say: 'Less is more'!"

Curiosity blunted the edge of my irritation. "What does that mean?"

"It means that you don't always have to put in every single little thing that happened. You can craft a story so that it's short and sweet — and packs an even better punch." She looked at me to see if I was getting it. I just shrugged and turned my head away. I'd decided that I was insulted.

I remained insulted for the rest of the evening and on into the next day. But by the time I came home from school, I was overflowing with things I wanted to share with my mother. She patiently listened to all my stories, even though there were a million and one other things — like her supper preparations, my little sisters, and the laundry piled in a heap on the dining room table — that required her attention. She did ask me to fold the laundry while I talked, which meant that I had to raise my voice and practically shout to reach the kitchen, where my mother was cooking. But I didn't mind. Telling my stories felt too good.

I'd recently discovered the joys of chatting on the phone, and that evening I spent at least two hours doing just that with various friends of mine. Later, at loose ends, I wandered into the living room, where Gavriel and Shimi were peacefully reading.

"Did I tell you guys what happened in my Geography class today?" I began, plopping down in an armchair so that they were facing me on the couch — a captive audience. "It was the funniest thing ...." And off I went, spinning out the tale for long minutes.

Gavriel's eyes kept going back to his book, but he didn't want to hurt my feelings by openly reading it. Shimi wasn't so polite. He pointedly ignored me, turning the pages of his book loudly to underline his message. I ignored his hints. The story was too good, and it was so much fun telling it.

Finally, Shimi put down his book and made the same chopping motion with his hand as he'd done at the table the night before. "Cut it short!" he begged. "Did you ever hear the expression, 'short and sweet'?"

I sat up, affronted. "For your information, I was almost finished," I said icily.

"So what happened next?" Gavriel asked, trying to keep the peace. His voice sounded tired.

"Who *cares* what happened next?" Shimi said. "In case you didn't notice, C.B., I'm trying to read here!"

I stood up. "I can take a hint," I sniffed, and flounced out of the room.

This time, I was *really* insulted. First my mother, and now my brothers. No one appreciated me! I went upstairs in search of sympathy and let myself be roped — without too much protest — into telling my younger sisters a bedtime story.

Their eager interest was a balm to my outraged spirit. Unfortunately, the story dragged on so long that when my mother sent my father upstairs to check if the girls were asleep, he found me still droning on to the drowsy-eyed little girls.

"C.B., this is taking way too long," my father said. "I think this can be finished up tomorrow night, don't you?" His voice held a gentle reprimand.

I waited for my sisters to protest, but they were silent. So I did it myself. "I was just coming to the best part!"

He smiled. "Look," he whispered.

I looked. My sisters were both fast asleep.

Even my little sisters found my stories boring! This — on top of my mother's advice, my brothers' lack of interest, and my father's rebuke — was the last straw.

I was *highly* insulted now, and I didn't care who knew it!

•◎•◎•

The offended feeling translated into a royal fit of the sulks, which lasted all through Shabbos and into Sunday. With my brothers at yeshivah until late in the afternoon, my parents decided to take my little sisters to the park. They invited me along, too, but I loftily declined. I didn't want to spend time with a family that wasn't interested in hearing what I had to say!

My sisters begged me to join them, but I stood firm. "Not this time," I said. "You two go on and have fun."

"What will *you* do today?" my youngest sister asked.

"Maybe I'll go over to a friend's house," I answered vaguely.

But I didn't go to a friend's house. I didn't go anywhere. When the others had left, I found that I was in no mood for company. I walked around the empty house feeling very sorry for myself. Eventually, I went to the backyard to continue feeling sorry for myself out there.

It was a glorious day, all blue sky and fleecy clouds and warm breezes. Most of it was wasted on me. I was in too grumpy a mood to appreciate the weather. Perching on a swing, I rocked gloomily to and fro. I told myself that I appreciated the solitude, but that wasn't really true. I was lonely. I wanted to talk to someone.

I had nearly made up my mind to go over to a friend's, after all, when a sound from the house next door made me sit up and listen.

It was the sound of someone calling for help.

There's no fence between our backyard and the neighbors', so there was nothing to stop me from running over there to see what was wrong. The voice I'd heard belonged to Frumi, the only girl in the Fink family.

Why was Frumi calling for help?

I stood in the middle of the Fink yard and looked around. There was no sign of her. There was no sign of anyone. Then I heard her call out again. "HELP!"

The voice was coming from the house.

Moving closer, I called, "Frumi? Where are you?"

"HERE! Is that you, C.B.? Help! Get me out of here!"

At last, I tracked her down to a small basement window. Crouching down to peer through the window, I saw Frumi gazing up at me from below. She was nine years old, but looked younger. Right now, her cheeks were stained with tears, which began gushing again the minute she saw me.

"What are you doing down there, Frumi?" I asked

in surprise. "Why don't you come upstairs?"

"N-nobody's home," she sobbed. "I was supposed to go to my f-friend down the block while my mother and f-father went shopping, but I ran back to get a game from our b-basement. My parents d-didn't know I was there … and they went out. And then the basement door locked, and now I'm s-stu-u-ck!" The sobbing intensified.

"Okay, just calm down," I said, while my brain tried frantically to come up with some way I could help her. "I'll check the doors."

A quick run around the house showed me that both the front and back doors were securely locked. There were no open windows, either, except for the basement one where Frumi was. "No luck," I admitted, crouching down to talk to her again. "But don't worry. I'm sure your parents will be home soon."

"Can't you get me out?" she asked pathetically.

"How?" I asked.

Frumi had no answer. The house was locked. "Can you climb out of this window?" I asked doubtfully.

"Too high," she said. "And even if I could reach it, it's way too small for me to squeeze through."

She was right. I saw her eyes fill again, and her chin begin to quiver. Quickly, I said the first thing that popped into my mind. "Want me to tell you a story while we wait?"

Her face lit up. "Will you wait with me till they come back?"

"Sure. So find something to sit on, Frumi, and make yourself comfortable. Here's the story …."

I started making one up, adding characters and new plot twists as I went along. After a while, I was enjoying myself so much that I almost forgot about Frumi. Then I saw her wipe away a surreptitious tear. The scared look was back in her eyes. I was losing her.

My mother's advice came floating back to me, from that place where advice patiently waits until you're ready to listen. "Less is more … Craft a story so that it's short and sweet … It packs a better punch!"

I decided to try.

Until that point, I'd been slathering details onto my story like syrup on pancakes. Much as it hurt to do it, I began cutting back on the wealth of detail, which made the story move along at a much brisker pace. I saw Frumi start paying attention again. The tears dried up. Her eyes shone with excitement. I was reaching the high point of the story when we heard a car pull into the driveway.

"It's your parents!" I cried jubilantly.

Frumi waved an impatient hand. "Great. But what happens next, C.B.?"

•◎•◎•

Everyone made a big fuss over me after Frumi was extracted from the basement. Her mother insisted on serving me cocoa and cookies, while her father praised me for staying with Frumi while she was locked in. But Frumi had only one thing on her mind. "Can you finish the story now?" she begged when I'd finished my snack.

Frumi's brothers wanted to hear it, too. Then and there, I gave them a quick summary of what had happened so far and then proceeded to the exciting climax and satisfying ending.

"Did you make up all that just now?" Frumi asked, awed.

I laughed. "It's what I do best."

Inside, with a grimace, I added: *According to my family, it's also what I do worst ….*

Our adventure spread up and down the block as if it had wings. When I babysat for a neighbor a couple of nights later, the kids begged me to tell them a story, "Just like the one you told Frumi." This time, I made sure to do it the right way, right from the start. Just enough detail to make it interesting, but not so much that it buried the story. Enough of a plot line to offer some real entertainment, but not so long as to put people to sleep …

They loved it. What's more — *I* loved it! For the first time, I was beginning to have a dim idea of what being a real storyteller is all about. It's a craft, like anything else. And, like any craft, it gets better if you take the time to think — *and* to prune away the unnecessary parts.

My stories and I gained quite a reputation on our block. And then, one day, a woman called me out of the blue and introduced herself as the sister of one of our neighbors. She asked if I'd tell a story at her daughter's bas mitzvah party the following week!

"M-me?" I asked disbelievingly.

"Yes! I've heard that you really know how to tell a good story. I'm willing to pay you nicely, C.B. What do you say?"

What else could I say but "Sure!"

"And that," Ma concluded, "was how I started my career as a storyteller."

"And now people call you up all the time and ask you to tell stories at schools, parties and other places," Rivi said, writing busily.

"Right. And now," Ma said, getting to her feet, "I really must get back to that recipe. How long will it take you to write up the interview? I'll need you to set the table soon."

"Oh, it won't take long at all," Rivi assured her sunnily. "I'm not in the mood to write a lot. Just a couple of paragraphs should do it."

"That's all?" Ma was surprised. "Isn't that a bit on the short side?"

Rivi grinned mischievously. "Well, you know what they say … 'Less is more'!"

"Somehow," Ma said, "I don't think your English teacher is going to buy that."

"I guess I can get away with it."

"And I guess *I* can get away with giving you only *one* of those cookies I'm about to bake …"

Rivi looked alarmed. "Okay, okay — you win. I'll do the job right."

"That," said her mother, "is the only way to do anything!"

And then, to cheer her daughter on as she went upstairs to tackle her assignment, she called after her, "I'll make that two cookies, Rivi. Even three, if you get the assignment done before supper."

"It's a deal!" her daughter's voice came floating back.

"*Hmm* … assignments," Ma murmured. "Getting by with the minimum … mothers and daughters …" She stood stock-still in the middle of her kitchen, with a look on her face that her family would have found very familiar.

By the time the delicious smell of cookies began wafting out of the kitchen and up the stairs to tickle Rivi's nose, it was time to say "*mazel tov*." Another story had been born!

Special Delivery

It was Nissan, the season of Pesach cleaning, and Ma had a special job for Binny and Ora.

"I want you to go out —," Ma began.

"Out?" Binny brightened. He had been rather gloomily contemplating a day spent scrubbing away indoors.

"— to Mrs. Greenbaum's house," Ma continued. "She could use your help today."

"But I thought Mrs. Greenbaum always goes to her daughter's house for Pesach," Ora said.

"She does," said Ma, "but she got into the cleaning spirit this year, and started emptying out her breakfront. Unfortunately, the exertion was too much for her and she pulled a muscle in her back. She needs your help to put things back in order for her."

Binny followed his sister out of the house, resigned but not unhappy. Cleaning someone else's house was a bit more interesting than cleaning his own. And Mrs. Greenbaum was a fantastic baker. Maybe there would be some of those yummy peanut-butter cookies ....

There were no peanut-butter cookies, but Mrs. Greenbaum did serve her young neighbors a slice of fresh chocolate cake apiece before they started working.

"Yum!" Binny exclaimed through a full mouth. "This is great! Our mother gives us a treat *after* we've done the job."

"I'm grateful to the two of you for coming over," Mrs. Greenbaum said with a smile. The older woman smiled often, but Ora had often thought there was something sad in her face at the same time. Maybe it was her eyes ....

Right now, those eyes were regarding her work crew in a friendly but businesslike way. "If you're finished ...?"

The children took the hint. Binny and Ora recited the *brachah acharonah* on the cake, washed their hands, and headed for the dining room.

The table was piled high with the contents of the huge old breakfront that graced one side of the room.

"Sorry about the mess," Mrs. Greenbaum said. "I haven't cleaned this thing out for at least ten years — since my husband passed away and I stopped making Pesach. I decided to finally do it this year. As you can see, I made a good start. I like to finish what I begin. Unfortunately" — with a small grimace, she placed a hand on her back — "that wasn't possible this time."

"No problem, Mrs. G.," Binny said cheerfully. "What goes where?"

Binny and Ora spent an enjoyable couple of hours sorting through a decade's worth of accumulated "stuff." Under Mrs. Greenbaum's direction, they moved things into various piles, to be saved or thrown out. When everything had been sorted to their neighbor's satisfaction, Ora set to work polishing silver while Binny started putting things back into their allotted drawers and cabinets. But first, he was given a cleaning spray and rag and told to wipe down all the drawers and cabinets on the inside.

He enjoyed the squirt-and-swipe routine immensely, and was sorry when he came to the last drawer at the bottom of the breakfront. As he reached inside to make sure it was empty, his hand encountered something stiff and square. It felt like a photograph. He pulled it out to make sure.

"A picture!" he called. "I found a picture wedged into the back of the lowest drawer!" He held it up to examine it.

In the photo, a teenaged boy was standing in between a man and a woman, all three of them beaming with pride. The woman looked like a younger version of Mrs. Greenbaum, and Binny guessed that the man was her husband. Which meant …

He held out the picture. "Is this your son?"

"*What?*"

There was a strange note in Mrs. Greenbaum's voice, but Binny didn't notice because he was busy turning the photo over to read what it said on the back: "*Avi's Graduation Day.*"

He'd just managed to make out the words when the

picture was snatched from his grasp. "Where did you find this?" Mrs. Greenbaum snapped.

Binny looked up in surprise. He'd never heard Mrs. Greenbaum sound like that before — sharp, as though her voice had turned into a knife that wanted to slash something up. "In the back of the drawer," he answered meekly. "Did I do something wrong?"

She caught herself. "No … no, of course not. I — I was just surprised, that's all." She glanced at the picture, and then looked away again, as if the sight hurt her eyes. "I haven't seen that picture in a long time. A very long time …"

"*Is* it your son?" Binny asked curiously.

There was a long pause before Mrs. Greenbaum answered. So long, that Binny thought she might never tear herself from whatever thoughts were absorbing her — and were clearly causing her a great deal of pain. Ora nudged her brother and shook her head slightly, as if to say, "Let it go."

Binny was perfectly willing to let it go. He wished he'd never asked the question in the first place. In fact, he wished he'd never found the picture, if it was going to make nice old Mrs. Greenbaum so sad.

"Yes," Mrs. Greenbaum answered at last. "He is my son. Though I very much doubt that he remembers that by now …"

•◎•◎•

"It's time for spring cleaning!" Mark's mother announced cheerfully as she threw open the windows to the gentle California breeze.

"Aw, not again," Mark groaned. But he did it mostly for show. He didn't really mind the annual spring cleaning, because it was kind of fun. All three of them — his mother, his father and himself — worked together and then went out for pizza afterwards.

"What do you mean, 'again'?" his father asked quizzically. "It's been a whole year, kiddo."

"Well, it feels like much less." Mark finished his cereal and took the bowl to the sink.

"Please pass the milk," his mother said, pouring coffee for her husband and herself.

Her words reminded Mark of something he'd been meaning to ask his parents. "There's a kid at school named Reuben, who's also Jewish, like me," he said. "And his parents aren't making him go to school all next week. It's a Jewish holiday, Reuben says. It's called, 'Passover.'"

There was silence at the table. Not the comfortable kind of silence, when people are enjoying their breakfasts and their own thoughts. The uneasy kind.

Mark looked from his mother to his father. "What's going on?"

"Passover …," his mother murmured.

"Pesach …," his father said, as though in a dream.

"So, can I stay home from school, too?" Mark asked eagerly. "I mean, I'm just as Jewish as Reuben is. Right?"

"We'll see," his mother said vaguely. Which usually meant that she wouldn't bring up the subject again unless he did.

Mark decided to try the old "fairness" ploy. "It's not fair!" he grumbled. "How come other kids get to have Passover, and not me? Aren't *I* entitled to a Jewish holiday, too?"

His father looked down into his coffee cup. "Yes, well …"

Mark waited. When nothing more was forthcoming, he demanded, "'Yes, well'? Is that all the answer I'm going to get?"

"Maybe we'll do something together one day next week," his mother said, with an attempt at brightness.

Mark remembered another grievance he'd been meaning to raise. "Reuben says his grandparents are coming to spend Passover with them. Why can't I ever spend time with *my* grandparents?"

"You know very well that Mom's parents are no longer alive," his father said quietly.

"Well, what about yours? You have parents, too. Don't you?"

"My father died years ago, Mark. When you were only a baby."

"And what about your mother?" Mark held his breath. Dad *never* talked about his parents. "Is *she* still alive?"

There was a long pause — so long, that Mark began to wonder if his father would ever say anything again.

"Yes," Mark's father said at last. "She's still alive."

"So why can't we visit her? I have a right to know my own grandmother, don't I?"

His dad looked away. "Yes, well …"

And that, it seemed, was that.

"He was such a lively boy," Mrs. Greenbaum said sadly as she and her young guests sat around her kitchen table taking a milk-and-cookies break from cleaning.

"You don't have to tell us if you don't want to, Mrs. G.," Ora said quickly. Her soft heart was touched by her neighbor's obvious suffering.

"I want to tell you. It's been such a long time since I talked about him to anyone." She drew a long breath. "About Avi …"

They waited expectantly.

"He was a lively boy," she began again. "Too lively, maybe. He was always up to something in school, and not paying enough attention to what he was supposed to be learning. We were hard on him, his father and I. Maybe a little too hard … Instead of becoming more interested in Torah and *mitzvos*, he seemed to become less so as the years went by. That picture" — she nodded at the photograph that Binny had unearthed — "is probably the last one we took when he was still living the kind of life we could approve of. We had it taken at his graduation from high school."

"And after that?" Ora prompted gently.

"After that, Avi went his own way. Instead of continuing on in yeshivah, he found himself a job in sales. Eventually, that job took him to different parts of the country. The last I heard" — her voice broke — "he was in California."

"That's sad," Binny said, the words sounding inadequate even to him.

The older woman nodded. "It *is* sad. What's even sadder is that he's dropped completely out of our lives. He — he was angry at us for rejecting him. *We* were angry at *him* for rejecting everything that we'd taught him. He came home for his father's funeral, and while I was glad he was there, seeing him brought back all the pain he'd caused us. There were words … a terrible scene … And then he left for the last time." She looked down at her hands. "I haven't seen or heard from him since."

The kitchen seemed suddenly too small for the three of them. Binny stared hard at the window, wishing he was outside in the yard, wishing he were anywhere but here, trying not to look at the nice lady from next door who was wiping away tears with the back of her hand.

"You never know," Ora said hopefully. "He may come back one day."

Mrs. Greenbaum gave her a tremulous smile. "That's true. You never know. And if he ever did come back, I wouldn't welcome him with the same anger anymore. I'd keep the door open instead of slamming it shut."

"We'll *daven* for Avi," Ora offered.

"Great idea!" Binny exclaimed, jumping to his feet. "Let's finish the job and go home and *daven* right away!"

With a shaky but genuine laugh, Mrs. Greenbaum got up, too. "I see you're anxious to be off. You should be through soon, anyway."

Ora shot her brother a baleful look for making his feelings so obvious. Ignoring it, he sailed through the kitchen door and back to the dining room, with its piles of stuff still waiting to be stored away.

There were piles of stuff everywhere. Usually, Mark enjoyed looking through things that he'd mostly forgotten about since the year before. Now, however, his mind was somewhere else. It was wherever his grandmother might be — the elusive grandmother who his father had said was still alive, though not a part of *their* lives. Why not?

At the bottom of a drawer, wedged in tight between some old restaurant menus, Mark found something interesting. It looked like a wedding invitation.

Opening it, he saw that the invitation was for someone called "Sara Greenbaum." Greenbaum — the same name as his! But who was Sara? He looked at the bottom, where the parents' names were listed. There it was again: "Mr. and Mrs. David Greenbaum."

Were they related to his own family? And what was that funny language on the opposite side of the page? His friend Reuben went to Sunday school and was learning to read Hebrew. Was this Hebrew?

He was about to run over to his mother to ask her, when he thought of a better plan. There was a small envelope tucked into the invitation, and the address on the envelope read "Mr. and Mrs. David Greenbaum," with an address in New York. There was even a stamp on the envelope already.

Mark hesitated, and then pulled out the return card. On the back, he wrote in his neat, careful handwriting:

"Hi! My name is Mark Greenbaum. Are you related to us? I don't know who's getting married, but congratulations, anyway! Love, Mark. P.S. Write back soon."

He sealed the small envelope and lettered the words "SPECIAL DELIVERY" on the front. Then he added another stamp to the one that was already there, just in case. He wanted to make sure his letter reached its destination.

It was only after he'd run outside to drop it in the mailbox that he thought of checking the date on the invitation.

The wedding — whoever's it was — had taken place eight years before.

Mrs. Greenbaum's dining room was back in order again, and so was her life. Over the next couple of days, she went about her simple daily routine: having her breakfast, making her phone calls, doing a little shopping. When she returned home on the second day, she found a small pile of mail inside her front door.

Scooping it up, she brought it inside to look at it over a cup of coffee. Bills … more bills … a letter from her granddaughter's school … an invitation to a friend's grandson's bar mitzvah … and a return card.

A return card? She frowned as she studied the small

envelope. It had the names of both herself and her husband on it, though her husband had died ten full years before. The envelope bore two stamps and had the words "SPECIAL DELIVERY" written across the bottom in what looked like a child's handwriting. What could this be?

Puzzled and intrigued, she slit open the envelope, pulled out the card and read the message on it.

And then she fainted.

Binny's mother had sent him over to Mrs. Greenbaum's house with a Pesach recipe their neighbor had asked for. Mrs. Greenbaum was going to her married daughter's house in a few days and planned to help with the cooking.

But his knock went unanswered. He knocked again, and then tried ringing the bell. Nothing.

He decided to go around back to the kitchen door. Sometimes Mrs. Greenbaum had the radio on in there, and might not have heard him at the front.

Sure enough, he could hear the radio playing when he arrived at the back door, but no one answered his knock there, either. The door was next to the kitchen window, and the shade was up. After a brief hesitation, Binny peeked inside.

What he saw made him start running back home as fast as his legs could carry him.

By the time Binny's mother arrived next door, Mrs. Greenbaum had come to. She was sitting up on the floor, a shaky hand to her head, when Binny's mother — followed by a very scared Binny — came bursting into the kitchen, using the spare key that Mrs. Greenbaum had once given them for emergencies.

Ma wanted Mrs. Greenbaum to go to the hospital for a checkup because she'd fainted. But Mrs. Greenbaum shook her head. "I'm all right. I just had … a bit of a shock." She held out the return card, which had remained clutched in her hand the whole time.

Binny read the message over his mother's shoulder. Then he looked at the envelope, with a return address in California. He looked wide-eyed at his neighbor. "Is this from your son?"

But Mrs. Greenbaum wasn't listening. She was at the phone calling Sara, the daughter whose wedding invitation had started this whole thing. There was so much she wanted to discuss with her.

How had this return card come to be mailed now, eight whole years after the wedding? Back then, her engaged daughter had insisted on sending an invitation to her brother Avi at his last known address, even though he hadn't spoken to anyone in the family for years. Mrs. Greenbaum and her husband had not really expected Avi to reply — but they had hoped.

In vain, as it turned out. All they'd received back was more of the same silence as before.

Most of all, she wondered this: Who, exactly, had penned the message on the back of the card?

The phone rang twice, and then her daughter picked up. Mrs. Greenbaum drew a long breath.

"Sara," she said quietly. "You're not going to believe this …."

It was Pesach night. At Binny and Ora's house, the Seder table had been beautifully set, with a Seder plate in the middle and a goblet at each place for the four cups of wine.

But the house next door was dark and empty. Mrs. Greenbaum was at her married daughter's home, where the table was similarly resplendent in honor of the special night.

Mrs. Greenbaum's daughter, Sara, had been busy this past week — and not just with cleaning and cooking. She'd been burning up the phone wires, calling a number that she'd never called before. And, in the process, a fire was lit in a place where coldness had reigned ....

Seated at the table along with Sara Greenbaum, her husband and their three children were Sara's mother, Mrs. Greenbaum ...

And Sara's brother, Avi Greenbaum.

And Avi's wife.

And their eleven-year-old son Mark.

Avi and Mark were wearing brand-new *yarmulkes* that Sara had bought for them. Mark kept reaching up to touch his, as though surprised to find it there. As for Avi, he wore his *yarmulke* with the familiarity and rising emotion that one feels when greeting an old friend after a long, long absence ....

As the goblets were raised for "*Kaddish*" to launch the Seder, Mark looked across the table at his grandmother. "Bubby," she'd urged him to call her.

Bubby. It had a nice ring to it.

He thought briefly about his home in California. It felt a million miles away — as if it belonged in somebody else's life. The life of someone who had no Pesach. No *yarmulke*. No Bubby ...

He looked at the words on the page of his Haggadah. "*Whoever is hungry, let him come and eat. Whoever is in need, let him come and celebrate Pesach.*"

Mark heaved a sigh of pure happiness. He fingered

his *yarmulke* and gazed around the table at this family he hadn't even known he had. And he basked in a warmth that he'd never even known he was missing.

It felt good to get out of the cold.

Yesterday

Mr. Davidowitz picked his head up from his *sefer* and listened. "Do you hear that?" he asked his wife.

Mrs. Davidowitz nodded. "It's pretty hard to miss."

"Sounds like World War Three up there."

With a sigh, Mrs. Davidowitz said, "No war. Just Vivi."

Vivi — as Aviva, their oldest, was known to family and friends — had just celebrated her thirteenth birthday. And her family was still reeling …

You'd think, Vivi's mother mused as she folded laundry, that maturity would bring *better* behavior. Somehow, though, things had moved in the opposite direction. The once-delightful little girl had turned into a far-from-delightful teenager. Her moods were erratic, her temper uncertain, her manner with her younger siblings brusque. Every now and then — like tonight — things got really out of hand. As her husband had put it: World War Three.

Mr. Davidowitz headed for the girls' bedroom to see what the trouble was. He found Shani in tears, Etti pouting, and their brother Mordecai hovering near the door, arms folded across his chest as though it would take a bulldozer to dislodge him. And right in the middle of everything was Vivi.

Their father addressed her first. "What's going on, Vivi? It sounded pretty lively in here a minute ago."

"I can tell you what's going on," Mordy volunteered. "Vivi stole my bag, that's what!"

"That's a pretty harsh accusation," Mr. Davidowitz said mildly. "Care to explain?"

"*I'll* explain," Vivi exploded, with a baleful look at her brother. "Mordy claims that he 'called' this bag for keeping his stuff in when we travel tomorrow. I told him that I *always* use this one when we go away. So Mordy and I have been having an argument about it."

"Why is Shani crying? And Etti looks pretty upset, too," her father wondered.

Vivi shrugged. "They got in the way."

"V-vivi hurt my f-feeeeelings!" Shani blubbered.

Her father gathered the eight-year-old into his arms. Over her head, he told the still-pouting Etti, "A word of wisdom: Never get in the middle of someone else's war."

"It's not a war," Mordy said. "I just want my bag back."

"*My* bag, you mean," Vivi snapped.

Mr. Davidowitz checked the clock on the dresser. "It's getting late. I wanted you all to be finished packing by now. We have an early start in the morning."

Suddenly, Vivi threw herself onto a chair in disgust.

"I don't even want to go. Why do I have to go, Abba? I'd rather be with my friends."

Her father looked surprised. "I thought you love going up to the summer house on winter weekends. There'll be lots of snow, and we'll build a fire in the fireplace …."

Vivi was tempted. Then she shook her head. "We'll just end up fighting," she said, indicating her siblings. "I need some peace and quiet."

Don't we all, her father thought wearily. "Well, I'm not going to insist that you come if you really don't want to. But we'll miss you, Vivi."

"I'll miss you guys, too. But I'd rather stay home."

Mrs. Davidowitz was called into consultation. After her first surprised reaction, she reluctantly acquiesced to her oldest daughter's wishes. If Vivi didn't want to join the family on their one-day vacation, they would not make her go.

Mrs. Davidowitz had mixed feelings at the prospect of a Vivi-less trip. On the one hand, Vivi would be missed. On the other hand, there was no question that — the way Vivi was these days — everyone was bound to have a better time without her ….

"I don't like the idea of you spending the whole day alone at home," she told Vivi. "Will you go to a friend's tomorrow?"

"Of course!" Now that she'd gotten what she wanted, Vivi's mood had turned sunny. "I'll go call Devorah right now." As she left the room, she threw a grin at her brother. "You can have the bag, Mordy."

"Thanks a lot," he muttered. "It was mine, anyhow."

But Vivi was too far away to hear.

She returned a few minutes later to report that everything was set. She'd spend the day at Devorah's and sleep over, too.

"That's fine. Though we're hoping to be home by nine," Mrs. Davidowitz said. "The kids have school the next day …."

The rest of the family would be setting out very early for the two-and-a-half-hour trip to their summer home. Vivi would sleep late and then mosey on to her friend's house.

And a good time, her father thought, would hopefully be had by all.

Until mid-morning, all went according to plan.

The Davidowitzes left on schedule, at seven a.m. Vivi slumbered on in the empty house until nine-thirty or so, when she opened her eyes, yawned, stretched and smiled to herself at the unexpected luxury of a day away from her annoying siblings.

It isn't easy being the oldest, especially when you've crossed the line into young adulthood and your siblings are still very much … well, kids. Everything they did these days seemed to get under Vivi's skin. And — to be fair — everything *she* said seemed to get under theirs.

All in all, taking this one-day break from her family seemed to be just what the doctor ordered. Vivi congratulated herself on the brilliant idea as she climbed out of bed.

An hour later, having dressed, davened and enjoyed a leisurely breakfast, Vivi went to the phone. She speed-dialed her best friend's number and waited.

"Hello?"

"Hi, Mrs. Perlman. Can I please speak to Devorah?"

"I'm sorry, Vivi. Devorah woke up sick this morning. Two of her brothers have had the flu, and I'm afraid she's caught it. She's running a pretty high fever and feels miserable."

"Oh! That's awful. Please tell her I said '*refuah sheleimah*,' okay?"

"Thanks. Have a nice day, Vivi."

"Bye."

Vivi hung up. She pictured Devorah lying in bed, feverish and achy, and quickly said a short chapter of

Tehillim for her friend's speedy recovery. Then she contemplated the rest of her day.

With Devorah out of the picture, Vivi was at loose ends. She could call another friend, but the prospect of spending the coming hours with anyone but Devorah did not really appeal to her.

What *did* she want to do? She examined her mood, and discovered that she'd like nothing better than to stay home. Relax, read a good book, eat whenever she wanted, even take a nap if she felt so inclined. A day without her parents around to criticize her, or her siblings to drive her nuts. A day to do exactly as she pleased …

A gift-wrapped present that had dropped unexpectedly right into her lap!

"I wonder how Vivi's doing," Mrs. Davidowitz murmured. Her kids were out playing in the freshly-fallen snow while she and her husband sat relaxing in front of the fireplace. After much effort, Mr. Davidowitz had coaxed some flames from the logs he'd piled there. In a few minutes, she planned to fix some hot cocoa for them all.

"I'm sure she's having a great time at her friend's house," Mr. Davidowitz said, poking at the fire and sending a shower of sparks up the chimney.

"*Mm.* I feel guilty saying this, but the day has been so peaceful without her around."

"True," he agreed. "She's at a difficult age."

Mrs. Davidowitz stifled a tiny sigh. She couldn't help missing the old Vivi, with her ever-present smile and infectious giggle. When was the last time Vivi had giggled with her family? These days, it felt as if she mostly snapped and snarled. The whole family seemed to get on her nerves ….

"Seems like only yesterday when a family trip would have been no fun at all without Vivi," she said wistfully.

"Give her time," her husband advised. "She'll grow out of this stage before you know it."

"Is that a promise?" she asked with a hopeful grin.

The front door burst open and a horde of children burst inside, rosy-cheeked, bright-eyed — and ravenous. Pushing her difficult oldest daughter out of her mind, Mrs. Davidowitz went to the kitchen to make that cocoa.

Vivi was having a fine day. The hours were like golden balls that she could toss into the air and juggle any way she liked. Or she could just decide to lay them down — which she did in mid-afternoon, when she decided to

take a little nap. Wrapped in a colorful blanket that her mother had crocheted, she curled up on the couch and was soon drifting pleasantly through dreamland.

She awoke hungry. She'd been planning to eat at Devorah's and hadn't planned any supper. Foraging through the fridge and pantry, she found macaroni and sauce and cheese. There was some salad, too. *Good enough*, she thought contentedly. In no time at all, she'd prepared a light meal and was eating it at the kitchen table with a book propped open in front of her. An hour ticked by in the quiet house.

Vivi wandered back to the couch and gazed out the window at the lengthening shadows. As the day drew to a close, she thought how weird it felt to spend an entire day not talking to anyone. She'd liked it fine for a while, but she had to admit it was kind of lonely. She'd be glad when she saw the car pull into the driveway and heard the commotion of her family tumbling inside with their bags and their snacks and their stories.

Now that she'd enjoyed some time away from them, her attitude toward her annoying siblings had softened. Really, they weren't so bad. Shani looked up to her, Etti was cute, and even Mordy was fun to be with most of the time. She looked out the window as darkness fell, and waited.

Time had never moved so slowly. It was silly to expect them back yet. Ma had said she hoped to be back by nine. It was now just after eight. She'd better do something to distract herself, or she'd go crazy!

But distracting herself, Vivi found, was not that easy. She'd already read for hours and was not in the mood for much of anything else. Not by herself. On impulse, she went to the phone and dialed Devorah's number.

"I'm sorry, Vivi," Devorah's mother said. "Devorah just fell asleep. Try again tomorrow, okay?"

"Okay," Vivi said mechanically. She considered calling another friend, but then gave up the idea. Once again, she wandered to the couch and glued her eyes to the dark street outside. When would they get home already?

An hour later, she was still wondering. And beginning to worry.

•◎•◎•

Mr. Davidowitz gripped the wheel and peered through the windshield in a vain effort to see more than ten feet ahead.

"Daddy, I can't see a thing except fog!" Etti announced.

"Me, too," Shani concurred.

“Me, three,” their father muttered. Aloud, he said with an attempt at cheerfulness, “Yep, pretty thick fog tonight, kids. We’ll have to take it slow.”

His wife threw him an anxious look. “Do you think we should pull over and wait it out?” she asked in an undertone.

“Only if we have to. I’d like to get us home tonight.” He hunched over the wheel and fixed his eyes on the road — or what little he could see of it in the dense white fog. A shiver of fear traveled up his spine. A fog this dense was not only unpleasant — it was dangerous. He murmured a silent prayer for a safe homecoming.

And on he drove, at hardly faster than a walking pace.

Nine-fifteen. Where were they?

Don’t worry, Vivi told herself sternly. What was a quarter hour, anyway?

But when the quarter hour turned into a half hour — and then an hour — she gave herself full permission to worry as much as she liked.

Where were they?

“I wish I had Devorah’s number,” Mrs. Davidowitz

fretted. "Then I could call Vivi."

"What's the point?" her husband asked. "She'd only worry. It's a good thing she's over at a friend's and doesn't have to know what we're coping with here."

"Here" was a rest stop on the side of the highway. The Davidowitzes had pulled into it when the fog became too thick for Mr. Davidowitz to drive safely. Perhaps, if they gave it an hour or two, the fog would lift enough to let them continue their journey home.

The kids were tired and cranky. Luckily, they'd eaten a good dinner before they set out, so no one was hungry. Mrs. Davidowitz cuddled Etti in her lap while Shani, beside her, leaned against her shoulder. Mordy was standing in front of the six-foot-high highway map, figuring out how many miles stretched between them and home.

Outside, the fog swirled gently, cold and white.

Vivi's heart thudded as worry turned to panic. What could have happened to her family? It was past ten o'clock!

She'd tried both her parents' cell phones, but couldn't get through. They must be in a place where there was no reception. The house that had seemed so friendly at ten that morning had a completely different appearance now. Vivi jumped at every little sound. Each time a car moved past her house, she raced back to the window to see if it was her father's. It wasn't.

When she got tired of pacing the rug, she planted herself at the window again, turning out the living room lights to block their reflection on the glass. Now she could see the street clearly — only there was nothing to see. Nothing but an occasional car that wasn't the one she longed for.

Other visions rushed at her. Scenes of horrific disaster … of overturned vehicles and ambulances sending their sirens out into the night …

Stop it! she told herself. *They're fine! They* have *to be!*

Suddenly, she flashed back to her fight with Mordy last night. How silly, fighting over which bag to take on a trip. She remembered Shani's tears and Etti's distress — and her parents' disappointment at yet another scene of friction in which she, Vivi, held center stage. What had she been thinking? Why couldn't she just chill out and keep the peace?

The trouble was, she hadn't been thinking at all. Just reacting … A headlight swept the street and Vivi's heart leaped up. But it wasn't their minivan. She sank back, fighting tears. She wished she could turn back the clock and make it yesterday again.

Yesterday, she'd been packing a few things in

anticipation of a day in the country with her family.

Yesterday, she'd been a carefree teenager, with her family safe and together all around her.

Please, she whispered. *Let it be yesterday* ....

Yesterdays don't come back, Vivi realized sadly. There's just a long, long row of todays, and if you mess one up, you don't get it back. No day is repeatable. Every day is a chance to get it right — before it becomes a yesterday that you might regret ....

As Vivi sat in her dark living room in her empty house, these thoughts were hard to handle — especially with the terrible fear that pressed upon her and made it difficult to breathe. She tried her parents' numbers again, with the same results. She had never felt so alone in her life.

Across the street, lights twinkled in a house. Down the block, she saw the same thing. Only *her* house was dark and deserted and full of scary imaginings.

Yesterday, her house had looked just like theirs ....

She must have dozed off, because the next thing she knew she was waking up with a crick in her neck and something soft on her face.

Blinking in confusion, she realized that the soft thing against her cheek was a hand. Her mother's hand!

"Ma!" She sat up so quickly that her head spun. "You're home!" She threw her arms around her mother and hugged her as if she'd never let her go.

Mrs. Davidowitz looked exhausted but happy. "Yes, we're home — finally," she said. "We got stuck in an awful fog and didn't get in until a couple of minutes ago."

Vivi tried to focus her bleary eyes on the clock. "What time is it?"

"Eleven-thirty."

"I was so scared …."

"Why aren't you at Devorah's? If I'd known you were home alone, I would've been worried about you."

Vivi explained about the flu. "I kept trying to reach you, but couldn't get through …."

Smiling, Vivi's mother gently disengaged herself from her daughter's arms. "Well, all's well that end's well. I think we could all use a good night's sleep. Can you make it upstairs?"

Vivi swung her legs onto the floor and rubbed her aching neck. "I'm a little wobbly, but I'll make it."

"Good. Daddy's already taken the girls upstairs. And Mordy practically sleep-walked up to his room!"

In short order, Vivi found herself in bed. Her mother tucked the covers around her, murmuring, "It's a cold night."

Just yesterday, Vivi would have been annoyed with

her mother for treating her like such a child.

Just yesterday, she'd been … very, very silly.

She wanted to say something but was too sleepy to figure out the words. But it didn't matter. Her mother leaned down and kissed her good night, and somehow that was better than any words could ever be. She was home, and her family was with her, safe and sound, and all was well with the world ….

"Good night," Mrs. Davidowitz said softly at the door. There was no answer. She turned around.

Vivi was smiling in her sleep.

Bais Yaakov—an Orthodox Jewish girls' school
Baruch Hashem—thank the Almighty
Bentch (Yidd.)—recite the Grace after Meals
Bli ayin hara—without [meaning to cause] jealousy
Bli neder—without promising
Bnei Yisrael—the Jewish people
Brachah—blessing
Brachah acharonah—blessing recited after food
B'tzelem Elokim—in the image of Hashem
Bubby (Yidd.)—grandmother
Chas v'shalom—Heaven forbid
Chesed—kindness
Chumash—the Bible
Daven (Yidd.)—pray
Eineklach (Yidd.)—grandchildren
Erev Shabbos—Friday
Frum (Yidd.)—religiously observant
Gemara—Talmud
Haggadah—book recited at the Passover Seder
Har Sinai—Mount Sinai
Hashem—the Almighty
Im yirtzeh Hashem—if the Almighty is willing
Kaddish—the first stage of the Passover Seder
Lashon hara—gossip
L'kavod HaTorah—for the honor of Torah
Ma'ariv—evening prayer
Mann—the food that fell miraculously from Heaven and sustained the Jewish people in the wilderness for forty years
Mazel tov—good luck
Middos—character traits

Mitzvos—Torah commandments
Modeh Ani—prayer of thanks recited upon awaking in the morning
Morah—female teacher
Nachas—satisfaction
Neshamah—soul
Niftar—passed away
Parshah—weekly Torah portion
Rashi—classic Torah commentator
Rebbi—Torah teacher
Refuah sheleimah—a complete recovery
Ruach—spirit
Sefer—Torah book
Seudah—festive meal
Shabbos—Sabbath
Shamayim—Heaven
Shema—fundamental Jewish prayer that declares Hashem's unity
Shevet—tribe
Shidduch, shidduchim—dating to find a marriage partner
Shiur, shiurim—Torah class(es)
Shul—synagogue
Siyum—celebration upon completing the study of a significant Torah work
Tehillim—Psalms
Teshuvah—repentance
Tzaddik—righteous person
Yeshivah—Torah school
Zechus—merit
Zeeskeits (Yidd.)—sweeties
Zeidy (Yidd.)—grandfather